CINDERELLA
AND HER SISTERS

IDENTITY, AUTHORITY, AND INHERITANCE

TOM BLOOMER

Print Edition ISBN: 13: 978-0-9996759-0-8

Scripture quotations taken from the New American Standard Bible® (NASB) Copyright © 1960, 1962, 1963, 1968, 1971, 1972, 1973, 1975, 1977, 1995

by The Lockman Foundation. Used by permission (www.Lockman.org).

Illustrations: Jean-Charles Rochat, Geneva, Switzerland (www. expressioncreative.ch)

First published in 2016 in French by JEM Editions, 1405 Pomy, Switzerland (www.jem-editions.ch)

Printed in the United States of America

CreateSpace Publishing
4900 LaCross Road
North Charleston, SC 29406

CINDERELLA
AND HER SISTERS

IDENTITY, AUTHORITY, AND INHERITANCE

TOM BLOOMER

Contents

Foreword

Some people talk a lot. With others, you sense a deep, hidden wellspring of wisdom, and you wish they would say more.

In person, Tom Bloomer can seem reserved—he is an introvert, after all (and he proudly defends this, his "people group"). But when speaking publicly, that deep, hidden well of wisdom begins to gush forth, and he can become intense, animated, and dramatic. His teaching is gripping, humorous, and full of insights he has mined—both from dwelling long with the "Cinderella" characters you will meet with new revelation in this book, and from his decades of ministry in the French-speaking world. Tom is a profound thinker, and he communicates with clarity and insight.

I have known Tom since he joined Youth With A Mission (YWAM) in 1972, and I have been deeply impacted by his teaching ministry. I often say that the times we hear God most clearly are when we gather together, intent on seeking to know Him more. I cannot tell you how often God has used Tom to bring understanding and "the word of the Lord" to our movement, as he has spent hidden time in preparation to hear God's heart.

His impact has been profound upon Youth With A Mission and the University of the Nations (UofN), where he has served as the International Provost for over a decade. He has an ability to take complex issues and simplify them, resulting in take-aways that are not forgotten. Just the mention of one highlight word will bring back a flood of understanding to all who have heard the message.

So it is with the "Cinderella" story. One way of describing the role of Youth With A Mission would be to say that we help people out of their brokenness and into their rightful inheritance in knowing and reflecting God to the world. This happens as we come to know the name God has given us; it happens through not giving into the image others would impose upon us; and it happens as we recognize that we are valuable and sought after by the Prince, because He sees who we are meant to be.

As we become captivated by the Cinderella story, we recognize that our minds need to be transformed to see ourselves for who we are designed to be, developing a new way of thinking, and understanding that there is a Book that is the manual for all of life.

You will laugh and think deeply as you read *Cinderella and Her Sisters*—and hopefully it will bring you to that place of having a renewed mind that leads to a truly transformed life.

Darlene Cunningham
Co-founder, Youth With A Mission

Introduction

Identity, Authority, Worship, and Inheritance

Princesses and princes should be more concerned about inheritance than just about any other area of their lives. But history and experience tell us that this is too often not the case. Often, royalty give up authority over their own lives to others and thus lose their inheritance. Usually, in these cases, worship is going to the wrong place—or rather, to the wrong person. Understanding the dynamics at work between identity, authority, inheritance, and worship will help us to gain authority and use it for good.

Identity

A common theme in Prince-and-Princess stories is their struggle to know their true identity. Sometimes it is masked by an evil being, as in the case of Cinderella; in other cases, it plays out in the person's story, as with Abigail.

Those who come to steal our inheritance know that if we fully realize our identity as sons and daughters of the Most High, we will be fully able to start meeting the conditions of authority necessary to claim our full rights in the Kingdom. So the inheritance thieves constantly lie to us about who we really are and are created to become, attacking our hope, tempting us to shame and to despise ourselves. We far too often settle for too little.

The angels are looking over the balcony of Heaven and asking, "When will the sons of Adam and the daughters of Eve wake up? When will they realize that what is written about them in the Book is really true? How long?"

These are the cosmic questions.

Authority

In its essence, authority is influence. It is not to be confused with force. Force is power used to make people do things or refrain from doing things. The best example of right authority is God's. He has the power to force people to do whatever He would like them to do, but He does not use it. Instead, He uses His influence to get us to do what we know is right, and to stop doing things that are harmful to ourselves and others.

In the personal realm, authority can be inherited, as is the case with royal families; or it can be the authority of competence, that is, expertise; or it can be the authority of vision, often translated through passion. Authority of position also exists; a schoolteacher or a government official uses this kind of authority.

In most nations, the only people allowed to exercise force are the police and the military. In the spiritual realm, authority is called faith. The New Testament promises believers authority over sicknesses, evil powers, problems, and weather. We gain spiritual authority through obedience, especially obedience to God. In other words, we have authority to the extent to which we are under authority (see Chapter Seven).

We need authority in order to enter into our inheritance. In rare cases, the authority of position may be sufficient, as when the child of a wealthy family inherits the family fortune. In many cases, however, authority of position is not enough. Inheritances are often contested, and other kinds of authority are needed in order to gain them.

Worship

Worship is woven into the fabric of the universe. God created all things, and originally everything gave worship to God. The angels, as personal beings, worshipped God fully and continually. They did so because He was the only being in the universe worthy of their worship. But then one of them, Lucifer, decided that he should receive the worship. One third of the angels decided to follow him, and they were all cast out of heaven, thereby losing their inheritance—whatever it was. We do not know their full story.

The next personal beings that God created were Adam and Eve. But He created them differently than the angels; He created them in His image. He placed them on earth and gave them the assignment of being stewards over the rest of creation. They received authority over it, and it was their inheritance. However, they decided to follow the serpent instead of God, thus directing their worship to the wrong being.

Then God, as the Just Judge of the universe, was obligated to exile them from Eden. They retained only shreds of their authority and were sentenced to win back their inheritance through hard work. Fatigue, sickness, and death also became part of their world, making their existence even more difficult.

Inheritance

What is our inheritance? It certainly includes "shalom," the Hebrew concept expressing not only peace, but well-being in every area of life. But this inheritance is not just health and material prosperity, as many Christians across the world believe. In a word, it is contentment, and so few of us have found it (see James 2:5).

Our inheritance includes the nations. The Messianic promise to the Son in the second Psalm is our promise also, as we are co-heirs with Christ (Romans 8:17). This means helping to be stewards of the nations, teaching them according to the commandment given us in Matthew 28:18-20. In this passage, we are told to go and teach the nations precisely because Jesus shares His own authority with us, and the authority of Heaven is crucial to our gaining this dimension of our inheritance.

Ultimately though, our inheritance is the Lord Himself. He has given Himself to us. He is ours, and we are His. We share in the Trinitarian unity, and we will see Him face to face throughout all eternity. Glory be to His Holy Name.

Dr. Tom Bloomer
Burtigny,
Switzerland
December 2016

1

Cinderella

Once upon a time, long ago and far away, a good King ruled over a peaceful, prosperous little kingdom.

Only one problem concerned the King: his son was not yet married, so the kingdom had no future heir. (Every person who thinks seriously about a kingdom must be thinking three to five generations into the future. True royalty never thinks just of themselves or their generation, or even just of their children.)

And so the King sent out invitations to all the kings he knew, telling them that if they were traveling in the direction of his kingdom, they were welcome to stay: especially if they were traveling with their daughters! And the kings were happy to respond, because of course each one wanted his princess to marry a true prince.

After each meeting with a visiting princess, once alone in their apartments, the King would ask his son, "What about this one? Wasn't she beautiful?"

And the Prince would answer, "Yes, Father, she was beautiful, and she was a nice person."

"Well?" the King would ask.

And every time, his son would give the same reply: "She's not the one."

So the King started to take the crown Prince on visits to neighboring kingdoms, to meet more distant princesses. They traveled farther and farther from their kingdom. But each time the Prince would answer,

"She's not the one."

"How will you know the one when you meet her?" the King asked at last.

"I'm sorry, Father, I don't know that," said the Prince. "But I am sure that when I meet her, I shall know her."

The King knew that his son was not trying to be difficult, and since the King believed in love, he wanted above all for his son to marry for love, not just for the duty of producing a future heir to the throne. But time kept passing, and the King grew increasingly concerned.

Finally the King came up with a different strategy. He called his counselors together and said to them, "Perhaps the princess my son seeks is right here in our own kingdom. After all, it's the only place we haven't looked. I will send an invitation to all the young ladies of the kingdom, calling them to come to a grand ball in the royal palace and dance with the Prince. Who knows? My son may find his princess closer than we think."

The King's counselors said that they thought this was a very good idea. (Of course, they said that about almost all the King's ideas. But this time it was certainly true.)

The Prince, always desiring to do the will of his Father, agreed to the plan. So the invitations were prepared and sent out, and the entire palace staff made ready for the great ball.

One of the invitations arrived at a big house located at the foot of the hill upon which the royal palace stood. The servant girl, seeing that it was addressed "To All the Young Ladies of the Kingdom," decided to open the large, heavy envelope sealed with the imprint of the royal ring.

She read within that all the young ladies were invited to a great ball to dance with the Prince, and in her heart, a spark of hope flared up. *I could have a place in the palace,* she thought to herself.

But just then, her two cruel stepsisters came up, and they snatched the invitation out of her hand.

"This invitation isn't for you!" they said. "It's only for us! You can't go to the palace and dance with the Prince; you're just our servant. Now help us get ready for the ball!"

And one of the saddest parts of this story is this: the servant girl accepted the lie. Even though deep in her heart she had believed that she could have a place in the palace, she shook her head with a sigh and chose to believe again the oft- repeated lie that she was only a servant—a slave, really.

Her life in the big house was very difficult. As the only servant, she had to do all the cleaning, the laundry, the cooking; she had to fetch the household's water and care for its fires; and she had to dance attendance on her two stepsisters and her wicked stepmother, who made her life even more miserable by endlessly ordering her around. Worse still, she had no room for herself; she was made to sleep in the corner by the fireplace, so that she was always covered with ashes.

But the saddest part of all was that she responded to the name her wicked stepmother gave her: *Cinderella.* That is no real name; it means "the girl who sits in the ashes." It was a false identity imposed upon her: a curse.

And it wasn't her true name. No loving mother would give her daughter a name that is really a curse. Cinderella's real mother had died long ago, and after a time, her father married a woman whose two daughters were as disagreeable as she was. The stepmother didn't really love Cinderella's father, but she married him because of his big house and his fortune. And she wanted to steal this inheritance away from Cinderella, to secure it for her own two daughters.

Then Cinderella's father died, too. And that was when she was told she could no longer sleep in her bedroom; that was when she became the servant of the household; that was when she started answering to the name that was not her true name.

Cinderella had forgotten her real name because she had forgotten where she came from. So she accepted the slavery of an imposed identity as her present existence, and she could not dare to believe that her true destiny was in the palace. She passively believed the lies.

She should have remembered—should have known better—because the story of her family was written down in an old Book. It told where her family had come from, about their responsibilities and rights, their authority, and especially about their wonderful inheritance. And it told the whole history of her family, which was full of examples of people trying to attack them, or trick them in order to steal their inheritance.

To be fair, the Book was not easy to understand. It was very old indeed, and it was not organized in a way that was easy to follow. There were songs, poems, histories, fantastic visions, proverbs, letters... and many, many stories. The family was very old, too, so the stories went way back into long-ago times. And there were dragons and sea monsters, princesses and concubines, emperors and kings, demons and angels, gods and heroes and traitors, wars and floods and famines and earthquakes, stars of the sky who at times seemed to be human...

Many parts of the Book just felt foreign to Cinderella, and not terribly relevant to her daily existence. She knew it well, and she still looked at it every day, because she loved to remember her father reading it to her. Reading the old stories gave her a kind of vague comfort. Unfortunately, though, the Book made no difference in her life, because she read it passively, as she did everything else in her life. She didn't read it as if it were true.

One day, a spiritual being came into her life and convinced her that she could indeed go to the ball. But because this supernatural intervention was not of God, it was truth mixed with a lie—as those not of God always are.

The true part of it was this: that she could go to the palace, participate in the ball, and even dance with the Prince. But the lie was that she could only stay an hour, since her place was not really there.

Cinderella was magically dressed in a beautiful gown, then went to the palace. As she entered, the Prince saw her, was struck by her loveliness, and asked her to dance. She heard the music of the best orchestra ever to play in the kingdom, danced with the Prince, twirled in his arms in the light of a thousand candles, looked into his eyes, saw the love awakening there…and still believed the lie. Because when the palace clock began to strike midnight, she broke away from the Prince, whirled on her heel, and ran off.

The Prince was so astounded that he lost precious seconds before reacting. Pretty girls usually didn't run away from him! By the time he reached the steps of the palace garden, she was gone. But he looked down and saw her slipper.

The Prince asked everyone at the ball who this wonderful girl was; nobody knew. But he had her slipper, so he vowed to try it on every girl in the kingdom, until he found the one it fit. Because this Prince was a prince of pursuing love.

This story is an ancient one; it existed for millennia before being trivialized by Walt Disney. A version of it was written down in China twenty-two centuries ago about a girl named Ye Xian, but long before that, it was told and retold in many different cultures. When I've asked those from Africa and Asia and the islands of the Pacific if they know the story, they say they have the same story, but she has a different name. In Indonesia, the story names a good sister (Bawang Putih, which means *garlic*) and a cruel one (Bawang Merah, which means *onion*). In Uzbek, her name is Shum-Shukkiz. In Korea, she is Kongji Patgi, the girl with the lentil basket.

Academic researchers have found versions of the Cinderella story told by the First Peoples of North America.

All the peoples of Europe told of the girl who lived in the ashes. In every European language—from Portugal in the west, through Russia in the east—her name is associated with ashes: the Germans told of Aschenputtel, the Dutch of Assepoester, the Afrikaans of Aspoestertjie, the Swedes of Askungen, the Norwegians and Danish of Askepot, the French of Cendrillon, the Spanish of

Cenicienta, the Portuguese of Agata Borralaheira, the Italians of Tchenerentola, the Romanians of Chenushareassa, the Finns of Tuhkimo, the Estonians of Tukatrinu, the Faroese of Oskufia, the Latvians of Pelnroushkita, the Serbs of Pepelyuga, the Ukrainians of Popelushka, the Bulgarians of Pepelyashka, the Russians of Zolushka...

It's a story as old as humanity, because God told it first. He tells it through the prophets; and in the New Covenant, He tells about His Son who awaits the preparation of the Bride, and of the wedding supper which is the culmination of history. It's our story, the story of all of us, and of the nations. We are all like Cinderella. Because the main source of Cinderella's problems is not her wicked stepmother and horrible stepsisters.

It is her mind.

How did Cinderella get to be so passive? After all, she was princess-born, with not just beauty and grace, but with the will power and initiative necessary to rule a nation.

I had wondered about this for years, and finally found out after my wife, Cynthia, passed away. Grief is a weight. It's like carrying around a loaded barbell. In addition, there is the fog of shock, and no desire to do anything, no energy. Cinderella first lost her mother. We aren't told when but possibly as a little girl or even at her birth. She was therefore even closer to her father, and adored him. Then when he announced he was going to remarry, and bring two more girls into the house, she must have gone through another time of grieving, knowing that she would now have to share him with others. Then, he died. It was too much. Her world had fallen apart. She didn't know what to do, where to turn. Her father had no close relatives (we know this because if they had existed they would certainly have come to check up on her). So in the end it was easier just to do what her shrill step-mother told her to do, hour by hour. She didn't have to think for herself. She couldn't . . . some are born with the tendency to passivity; others become that way through grief or extreme stress.

The passivity she had fallen into led her to accept the lie that she didn't belong in the palace. She'd forgotten where she came from, didn't know who she was, accepted a false name which was really a curse, and couldn't believe in her destiny even when she began to live it.

Cinderella is the perfect picture of a passive princess. And when you speak to her, she always has one answer: "Whatever you want."

You see, she could have broken out of her sad existence.

Everyone in the Kingdom would have known exactly where the Prince was trying on the slipper that day. His travels from town to town would have been the main topic of conversation. Why didn't Cinderella just drop her mop and bucket and run to the village where the Prince was?

Why? Because she had accepted the identity imposed on her by her wicked stepmother: that of the Ash-girl, with no past, nothing in the present, and no future. Although she occasionally thought of the palace and dreamed of being in it, it was no more than an escapist fantasy, a few stolen hours at a ball—she did nothing to actually live there. Her inheritance was being stolen from her while she watched, and did nothing.

However, the Prince had not a passive bone in his body. He kept looking, going from house to house and trying the shoe on each girl in the Kingdom.

We all know that after many trials and tribulations, and after her wicked stepmother and stepsisters do everything they can to keep them apart, the Prince finally gets to try the shoe on Cinderella. And she's the one!

The story usually ends just after that, with Cinderella being taken to the palace and being given a long, lovely bath by the ladies-in-waiting... then another bath, and another, until finally she stops smelling like the ashes of her former life. Cleaned and newly clothed in royal attire, she formally meets the royal family, the court, the palace staff. And she and the Prince marry and live happily ever after.

Except they don't, right away. (The stories rarely tell this part.) Oh, they are happy enough together, but the wedding has to be postponed for a while, because the King, so happy that his son the Prince has finally found his Princess, immediately sits down for a talk with his future daughter-in-law. And after just a few minutes of conversation he realizes that that this girl is not ready to reign over the Kingdom at his son's side. She has the position of a princess... but she doesn't think like a princess. She thinks like a servant, even like a slave. In her former life, she never thought for herself; she just did whatever she was told.

She did not know how to think about the prosperity and trade policies of the Kingdom, because she had never made financial decisions for herself. She could not assess the school system, the water systems, the legal system, defense and foreign policy, food production, care for the sick and infirm. She had only ever thought of herself and her small problems, and of how to get through her day. She was not at all ready to rule with the Prince.

Happily, in the second city of the Kingdom, there was a wonderful campus called the University of the Nations, where the Princess could get teaching on how to think. (I bet you've never heard *this* part of the story! You won't find it in most versions.) She began with the introductory course of this University, called a Discipleship Training School (DTS). She received lots of teaching to correct her self-image. Then she had to work on forgiving her wicked stepmother and two cruel stepsisters. Then she started courses on How to Think Like Royalty.

After a few months of this intensive training, the Princess realized herself how much she had to learn. She had come a long way from her chimney corner, but she now knew how far she still had to go. So after a lot of thinking and many tears, she asked the Prince and the King to postpone her coronation as Princess of the Realm until she understood better how to rule and reign with him. She and the Prince got married right away after that, but her title was Consort of the Crown Prince... for the time being.

So after getting her B.A. degree from this wonderful University, she attended a graduation ceremony with some of her fellow students and received a diploma signed by the President and Provost, as well as by the Dean of the Department of Ruling over Kingdoms. The coronation ceremony followed just afterward, and she ascended to the throne at the right hand of the Prince, who became King in the same ceremony. And then they lived happily ever after, had many children, and opened university campuses in other nations too.

That's a good story, isn't it? Even if you've heard it before. Because even the oldest story in the book, the one that Hollywood and Bollywood have made and remade and reversed and switchbacked and twisted a thousand times, can grip and hold the most skeptical or jaded of us.

Why is it that this oldest of stories strikes such deep chords in our souls?

Because every human being dares to hope that life can be better. We know we were not made for misery and despair. We were created in the image and likeness of the Most High. Then our inheritance was stolen away, and our beautiful garden became a vale of tears.

But we suspect that we are really royalty. Some of us know that our story truly does have a happy ending, in which we will attend the wedding supper of the Lamb, the Prince of Peace, and will rule with Him as His Bride as He wipes every tear away, in the place of absolute light, profound peace, incredible beauty, and infinite love.

Our basic problem, like Cinderella's, is passivity. Because people who are passive can be dominated, or stolen from, with very little effort. If you want their inheritance, just work first on making them passive, and stealing it will be easy. The ultimate theft is that of "true identity". If a thief can make you forget your own identity, then he can impose a different identity on you, and you won't even recognize that the inheritance is yours. Then the thief can steal it while you watch… and even get you to help him with the theft!

We have an Enemy who has been trying to steal our inheritance for thousands of years. He is a thief, a liar, and even a murderer. His job description is to steal, to kill, and to destroy.

But his power and knowledge are limited. He cannot resist the Most High and His warrior Princes and Princesses. The Most High gave His people the means of acquiring great wisdom; knowledge beyond measure; shining bonds of unity that make His holy army invincible; and weapons that cannot be resisted. And He gave them a Book, a Book of Books, that explains how all of this works.

There is a major key: to regain their inheritance, they must believe the Book and act upon what it says. Once they are wielding their celestial weapons in unity, no force in the Universe can stop them.

The Enemy knows this, and fears it. His armies are limited and weak in comparison; so they work a lot with lies, bluffing, and intimidation.

But this old Enemy has a strategy which has worked effectively for millennia to neutralize the Armies of the Most High. It is to lead them into passivity. His lies make them doubt the truths of the Book, especially the ones about their identity and their inheritance. He is always working to keep them focused on themselves, and uninterested in the greatness of their Kingdom inheritance: in time, in wisdom, and among the nations.

This Enemy leads us into passivity in many ways.

Take Cinderella for example. Many people have experienced what Cinderella did: accepting an imposed identity. An authority figure decides what we should study, or what we should do, or how we should act in a certain area. Sometimes this is done with good intentions, but it stunts our growth as persons. People who have a tendency to be passive anyway just go along with it to avoid conflict. For example, some of us have been told things like this in school or at home: "You're stupid! You'll never succeed! You're a failure!" As these kinds of remarks are repeated, they sink into our souls and become curses, holding us back from reaching our full potential. Inferiority complexes are terrible things.

Even things which are positive, such as being pushed to go to a certain university or join a certain profession, can lock us into identities that are not truly ours. One girl realized she had always and only done what her parents and older sister had suggested. She said, "I've been sitting back and watching a DVD of my life."

Are you a watcher? Or are you active in owning your choices?

Passivity can also be cultural. Cultures vary in the level of personal initiative they expect and encourage. In some Scandinavian cultures, individuals are not supposed to stand out; the saying is, "the heads of the tall poppies will be cut off."

The trendy term for this is "entrepreneurial"; just how much does the culture, and therefore the government, encourage the formation of new businesses? Some nations believe that government should be more active, and therefore the people can be relatively passive.

People from traditional cultures, particularly those that do not believe in time being linear, can be very passive. A friend was trying to get the people in his town in the Sahel to plant mango trees in their courtyards for the food and the shade; the response he received from almost everyone was, "If a mango tree is supposed to grow in our courtyard, it will grow there."

Passivity is often gender-based. In most cultures of the world, women are seen as the more passive gender, males as the active ones, even though passivity is a trap into which both men and women can fall. As girls and boys grow up, cultures like these implant "scripts" in them, training girls to behave more passively and boys to behave more actively. In some countries today, women are not permitted to start a business or even drive a car.

Passivity can be age-based. In some cultures, the younger people are expected to submit to the decisions of their elders. In others, the elderly can be relegated by their culture into the place of passivity. In a related way, passivity can come through the domination of one person over another. Some children are totally dominated by one or both parents.

In cases of abuse or family conflict, children can begin to retreat into a fantasy world. It's too dangerous where they live, so in an attempt to survive, they go somewhere else in their minds where it's peaceful. This is not wrong: it is a normal, God-given coping strategy that the mind implements to attempt to protect itself in a desperate, horrible situation, and victims of abuse are not to be blamed for this. In severe or prolonged cases of abuse, these mental habits of self-protection can become ingrained, leading to a loss of contact with reality. The long, slow work of unlearning habits that once protected you in extremity but now hinder your growth is incredibly hard and deserves the respect and full support of the people of God. In undertaking this work, abuse victims are often the strongest and most courageous of us all.

Some middle children have been found to be passive, as they end up being mediators in the sibling rivalries between the strong, oldest child(ren) and the baby of the family.

Introverts can be passive, also. As they are more likely to be observers, they can be tempted to leave action to others and to lose themselves in thinking or reading. Reflection is good, but if it never spills over into action, it is useless.

Passivity can be induced by drug use. With opium, the passivity was so extreme that it led to death. But even with milder drugs, such as marijuana, motivation can be destroyed as users talk more and more and do less and less. Exaggerated use of alcohol also has this effect.

Traditional churches have fostered passivity, with the priest or pastor being the actor in the worship service, and everyone else sitting there and receiving. Some churches broadened the actors to include elders and deacons. But women were often required to be passive in church. Happily, newer churches are finally showing that the priesthood of every believer can be a reality.

Passivity can come through theology. A false understanding of the sovereignty of God has led certain groups to believe that God has done and is doing everything in the world. So they conclude that prayer doesn't really change anything except the one who prays, and that evangelism isn't necessary, nor is a commitment to missions. The results of this thinking are: No evangelism, and little enthusiasm for prayer, since prayer doesn't "do" anything. For example, William Carey, who is seen by many as the father of the modern missions movement, proposed in a gathering of English pastors that missionaries be raised up and sent to India. One of them replied, "Brother Carey, if the Lord wishes to convert the heathen Indians, He will do it without our help." If William Carey hadn't broken out of the passive stance of waiting for God to do everything, then who knows when missions would have begun again? Besides, the Lord probably does not appreciate us expecting Him to do things He has already told us

to do… such as present the Gospel to every person!

We were created in the image and likeness of God, and as such, we were given authority to be stewards of all Creation (Genesis 1:26-27). The Lord wants us to be in action with Him; we are His co-heirs, with Jesus Christ.

Even in our personal lives, the implications of these truths are many. For one, we cannot just sit around and wait for healing or deliverance from depression or oppression. Of course we are to have faith, but "faith without works is dead" (James 2:20). If we are praying for healing, we need to be asking if there is anything we should be doing about it. Eating the right foods? Going to see a doctor? Going to the elders to ask for prayer?

One YWAM leader noticed that DTS teams were always asking for prayer because of fatigue. She finally responded, "If you're feeling tired, then your body is telling you that you need more sleep! So don't ask me to pray for you, just get more sleep! When you're hungry, do you ask for prayer because you're hungry, or do you eat something?" The answer in this case was action, not prayer.

Many are passive about their personal safety. They think that if they have faith in God, nothing bad will ever happen to them. Then when something bad does happen, they are astonished! We are taught that people who have a lot of faith can be flogged, stoned, imprisoned, or sawn in two (Hebrews 11:36- 38). Of course, in this same passage (v. 33-34), faith is shown to be a source of deliverance, also. But it is an active faith, a leaning into God, a faith based on obedience.

We must not forget our Enemy, the one who wants to steal, kill, and destroy. If we are effective for the Kingdom, he will try to stop us. Many accidents and diseases can be avoided if we are actively prudent, and if we specifically ask for protection in prayer.

Just knowing the promises of God does not help; they must be seized by faith (Hebrews 11:33). Just reading the Bible will not help us; we must allow the Word to read us. It must be appropriated, actively believed, and acted upon.

Another symptom of religious passivity is thinking that God guides us mostly through circumstances. According to this view, since God is in control, the circumstances around us are of His doing—or at least, by His permission—so they constitute guidance for us personally.

For example, if we're invited to join a missions trip and have no money, we could think that was guidance not to go. But the Bible is full of examples of circumstances not being according to God's will! People, spirits, even institutions, can all be in disobedience, and their disobedience can create circumstances that block God's will for our lives.

One of the promises to the Church is that the gates of Hell cannot hold against it. This means that part of the job description of the Church is to be breaking down Hell's walls! One reason prayer is given to us is so that God can work through our active prayers to change circumstances that are hindering us.

Passivity is one reason many Christians have problems exercising spiritual gifts. They think that prophesying, for example, means that God will somehow take over their tongues and make them speak. But that's not how the Lord works. He always invites us, and it is up to us to respond. In the case of prophecy, we receive a burden, an impression. New thoughts go through our minds, and it is up to us how to express them: as a prayer, or conversationally, or in the fashion of a prophet —that is, in a Christian meeting, with a loud voice, etc.

Passivity can infect our relationships. In marriage, or friendship, or professional contacts, if we do nothing, the relationships will sicken and die. Or in some cases, they won't ever begin.

The culture of victimization contains a large element of passivity. Blaming my problems on someone else is a very old practice; Adam tried it in the Garden. If we try to believe that "the Devil made me do it," or my culture, or my parents, etc., we'll never be able to get completely free of problems. We can be tempted to become passive about sin in our lives, just to live with it and never root it out. Individual responsibility is important to God! (See Deuteronomy 24:16, Jeremiah 31:29- 30, and Ezekiel 18.)

It's too easy to give up on the problems of the world, or even of our neighborhood. We can let ourselves be overwhelmed by them and become passive in the face of great need. We must constantly remind ourselves that God wants us to partner with Him and unlock His limitless resources. He will do the impossible if we commit to do the possible.

However, we must beware of the reaction against passivity: going to the opposite extreme, and tipping over into independence. Many women, upon awakening to the ways that their cultures have forced them into passivity, rightly rose up and insisted that they be allowed to exercise their God-given abilities in all areas of their lives. But as with all people who have been oppressed, there can be a temptation to move beyond rising up and into retaliation. This same phenomenon can happen when certain young people react against parents and other authority figures. To rise up and claim your place as an active agent in God's Kingdom is good; to lash out and retaliate is not.

So the false paradigm is of passivity swinging to independence. The correct one, though, is a right dependence coupled with initiative.

What does this mean? Here's an example: a friend of mine traveled a lot to speak in different conferences and seminars, and when a fellow passenger on the airplane would ask him, "What do you do?", he would answer, "I'm a Bible teacher." That would usually shut the conversation down. My friend finally realized he had to come up with a different description of what he did. So he had a business card printed up that said, "Intergalactic Enterprises" (this was before the Star Wars films). The card was big, shiny, and black, with reflective diamonds on it.

The next time someone asked him what he did for a living, he gave them a card. The conversation would go something like this:

"Amazing. Is your company really intergalactic?"

"Well, we're not there yet, but we have concrete plans to expand out to the other galaxies, yes."

"What does your company do?"

"We're very big in publishing—we have the number one all- time bestseller; we supply food on all continents and to all animals, too; we have large mining interests, especially silver and gold and precious jewels; and we're into education and healing in big ways, too."

"How is it I've never heard of your company?"

"Oh, it's a family-owned company, that's why it's not listed on any stock exchange. My Father founded it, and He's still running it."

"I've never even seen an article about it."

"My Father is hard to interview. He's a very good listener, though, once you make the effort to find Him."

"What do you do in the company?"

"I travel around and teach the company values and procedures. But I didn't start out that way. All of my brothers and sisters were raised the same way: our Father would give us a little responsibility in the family business; then if we were faithful with that, He would give us more. And the ones who are the most responsible are helping Him run things now."

My friend could go on like this for a long time. After a while, he would let his conversation partner know that the family enterprise he was a part of was the Kingdom of God! The other person would be fascinated, never having heard the work of God described in terms like this.

Here's the point: God wants us to grow in responsibility. So we depend on Him heavily when we first start out. But He also wants us to use our minds, which He gave us. So He is delighted when we take initiative; even in the Garden, He gave Adam the task of naming the animals. Adam had to decide!

Even after serving Him for decades, we should still check in with Him very regularly, even in routine situations; and when something out of the ordinary comes up, we need to press in for detailed guidance. This is not passivity, it's a close relationship with our Father. What a privilege!

Ask yourself, in which area(s) have I been passive? We all need a regular passivity checkup. Even if we have victories, we can too easily slip back in to passivity.

Sometimes a hurt or a failure can cause us to retreat back into passivity. How can we know? Ask the Lord!

2

Esther

Once upon a time, long ago and far away, an evil King reigned over a huge kingdom. And he needed a Queen. So he asked his seven royal counselors how to go about finding one.

They had been anticipating his request, because he had just banished the previous Queen. They proposed that the King's officers in every province find the most beautiful young ladies, carry them off by force and bring them to the palace, and prepare them to be shown to the King. Now this King was a cruel and absolute ruler, as well as being unthinkably wealthy. He did not look for true royalty in the character, where God does, but instead cared principally for appearance.

So throughout the land, the King's soldiers forced young women from their homes, their families, their communities, and brought them to the women's wing of the Kings' palace. One of the girls who was captured was a refugee, an orphan whose parents had died while her people were being sent away into exile. She was being raised by her uncle in the capital city of the kingdom, and her uncle's house was not far from the royal palace.

Perhaps you know this story, which can be found in the great Book. Though many of our modern retellings of this tale make it sound like a romance, in truth it is a tale of oppression and danger. It shows the hidden hand of God acting through the courage of a young teenage girl named Esther, who risked her life to save her people.

Esther did not want to be taken away from everything she knew, imprisoned in the palace, and raped by an evil King (though at the time the concept of "rape"—or sex by force, a great sin in the eyes of God—may not have been used). Who knew if she would ever see her home and family again? Everyone knew what had happened to the last Queen, whose only crime had been standing up for herself. This young girl still felt very much like a foreigner, and she was only fifteen years old.

The official in charge of the women's wing, Hegai, had served the King his entire life, as had his father and grandfather before him. And when he saw Esther, he knew immediately that she was the future Queen! She had been chosen for shallow reasons—because of her beauty—but unlike the King, this official recognized the signs of true royalty: her strength of character, and her graciousness to everyone around her. So he put Esther in the best place in the harem, and he gave her seven serving maids from the palace of the King.

Even though the candidates were the most beautiful young ladies of all the 127 provinces of the kingdom, they were not ready to meet the King. Meeting with royalty demands preparation and training. When that royalty is true royalty, the preparation and training are of the character. But this King was focused on looks.

So Hegai required of each girl twelve intensive months of skin-deep preparation: six months with oil of myrrh for their skin, and six months with perfumes and cosmetics.

Now, if this had been a romance, perhaps instead of all this abduction and coercion, the King would have thrown a ball, issuing invitations throughout the kingdom. He would have given young women the choice to come or remain home, and he would not have used them for his pleasure as though they were disposable, when in fact each and every one of them was a daughter of the King of Heaven. But this King commanded that, at the end of their year, each girl could request anything she liked for the night the King raped her. "She has only the one chance to make an impression," he said; "if I do not remember her name, she remains in the second harem." Since the King was wealthy beyond imagination, any girl could ask for literally anything: an orchestra, a circus, a banquet, a magician... whatever could make an impression.

When Esther's turn came, what did she feel? Did her heart fill with dread and terror? She knew there was no escape; if she tried to flee, she would be caught, and who knew what sort of punishment the King would rain down upon her, her family, her people? Did she have the sense that God was with her, no matter what fate befell her? Did she have a divine premonition of her calling, which the Lord often gives to His children? Was she visited by a regal confidence: "I've got this!" Perhaps it was all of the above. The story does not tell us.

She asked only what Hegai recommended to her, which was nothing.

The story tells us that the evil King loved Esther more than all the other women, and she won his grace and favor more than all the other virgins. Her true royalty was clearly apparent, even to a man such as him. So he set a royal diadem on her head and made her Queen (Esther 2:17).

After that, an evil prince hatched a plot to exterminate all Esther's people and steal their inheritances. Uncle Mordecai exhorted Esther to go to intercede with the King and to plead with him for her people.

But Esther was shocked at this request. Even though she was Queen, because of how cruel and dangerous the King was, she had no say in her own life or in how the kingdom was run. To challenge the King on anything was a perilous proposition, and he was notoriously inconstant in his moods and decrees. A courtier who was his favorite one week could fall out of favor and be banished or beheaded the next. She sent this reply to Mordecai: "All the King's courtiers and the people of the King's provinces know that if any person, man or woman, enters the King's presence in the inner court without having been summoned, there is but one law for that person—that they be put to death. Only if the King extends the golden scepter to the person may they live. And I have not been summoned to visit the King for the last thirty days."

Mordecai was unhappy with Esther's response, since he knew the laws of the palace very well. He knew that he was asking his niece to risk everything, including and especially her life. But she was going to lose her life anyway!

So Mordecai sent his answer immediately: "Do not imagine that you, of all the Jews, will escape with your life by being silent in the King's palace. On the contrary, if you keep silent in this crisis, relief and deliverance will come to the Jews from another quarter, while you and your father's house will perish. And who knows? Perhaps you have attained royalty for such a time as this."

Esther was shaken this time. It's true that during her time in the palace of the King, she had been cut off from her people. She lived in the palace as in a prison, not free to come and go. She was only permitted to keep company with the other concubines in the harem, and they were always under guard. Uncle Mordecai's response brought her back sharply to the reality of her people's persecution.

During that afternoon, Esther went from being a prisoner to becoming a True Queen. She responded to her uncle: "Go, assemble all the Jews who live in Susa, and fast on my behalf. Do not eat or drink for three days, night or day. I and my maidens will observe the same fast. Then I shall go to the King, though it is contrary to the Law, and if I am to perish, I shall perish."

So Mordecai went about the city and did just as Esther had commanded him.

Do you want to know if this story had a happy ending? Well, you'll just have to go read the original version, in the Book of Books. Because one of the Books is named after Esther the True Queen.

Esther's life has a message for many people today. They face at least two major traps in their lives: one is the Cinderella Temptation, which is to prefer to do what others dictate, to live passively under imposed identities. But the other is the Esther Temptation, which is a danger especially for the ones who are not passive but talented, educated, attractive, or in positions of privilege or influence. Sometimes people like this have had successes in life and are prepared for more. They see how they could have a greater and greater influence on the lives of the people around them. They are doing well. Sometimes, as in Esther's case, they live in dangerous times, without the protection of just laws.

And yet, when an opportunity comes up to risk all, even to possibly save an entire people, they hesitate. Why risk the good things they have, for the uncertainty and even danger of something that could turn out very badly? Or if (as with Esther) they live precariously poised between life and death, at the mercy of a cruel leader, why should they risk their own slim safety?

The area I have seen this in is missions. People come, get a taste of it, start to see what they could do for the Kingdom, and then hesitate. Leaving one's home country, raising support, learning another culture and language: all these challenges are huge. They think, *Why not just go home and get a good job? Have a ministry in a local church? Influence the people in my workplace?*

There's nothing wrong with this kind of plan, of course. Esther did not have the choices many of us have today. She could not have stayed at Uncle Mordecai's; she was abducted and held in the palace of the King. She could have let this paralyze her to any future action, saying, *Surely I have suffered enough!* And who could blame her? Yet when the moment came, when her nation was in peril, she rose up and offered herself to God.

And defeated the evil King. And saved her people.

Many times in the history of the Church, one person's courageous obedience has led to the salvation of many. And often, they were a young person. Esther moments are coming again. Will you be ready, when yours comes?

If Esther's story had been a fairy tale romance, rather than the tale of danger that it was, we can re-imagine the story with some very important principles concerning God's love for all peoples. As I said in the introduction, there's a difference between authority and force. King Ahasuerus knew all about force; he was a master at using his power as king to make other people do what he wanted. But in doing so, he was not exercising the authority of true royalty, as God models for us. King Jesus does not force; He invites. He has sent us with His message of love, forgiveness and redemption, and there are three stages to the communication of this message.

The first step is getting out the invitations. The evil king chose to take the young women away by force, but in God's Kingdom, no one is coerced against their will. For His wedding feast, He issues invitations. This we call evangelism, but we could say, quite biblically, that it consists of talking to people about the wedding supper. Many have heard of God; many also have heard that He had a Son, Jesus. But most have not heard that the Son is the heavenly bridegroom, and that He is awaiting the bride so that the wedding supper can begin. Even fewer have heard that they are invited! There's a place for each one at the table, with each name there. All we have to do is say yes to the invitation… and attend the longest, most glorious party in the history of the universe.

The second step in missions is getting them into the House of the King. Unlike the evil king's palace, where women were imprisoned, God's House is the Church, open and free. That doesn't necessarily mean a square building with a steeple, but it does mean two or three people meeting together regularly for prayer, worship, fellowship, and reading the Word together. We call this step, church-planting. It is an essential stage and the one we've been concentrating on in the most recent generations.

But missions doesn't stop there. There's another step, and it's crucial! Because the bride is not ready to meet the King. She needs intensive, long-term preparation to be able to reign with the King. For the king in the Esther story, this only went skin-deep, and we know that in God's eyes, "charm is deceptive and beauty is fleeting" (Proverbs 31:30). In the true Kingdom, the preparation is completely different. The Apostle Matthew calls it "discipling the nations" (Matthew 28:18-20).

In many ways, it's the most exciting step. It's where we see individuals helped and nations impacted by the Good News. It's not just about reading history but about making history. It's helping the nations to prepare for that glorious day when they will stand before the throne of the Ancient of Days, redeemed, purified, their cultural treasures with them, united in their diversity in the worship of the Most High and of the Lamb who stands in the midst of the throne. The Apostle John had an incredible vision of this crowning moment of our history and wrote it down for us to read in his Revelation.

Let's work and pray for that day to come!

3

The Prince

Once upon a time, long ago and far away, a Princess was born. But her family didn't know she was a Princess (which is often the case in these stories). The family was poor and didn't have enough money to feed the children they already had. And they didn't value girl babies nearly as highly as they valued boy babies.

So they did a terrible thing. They threw her out into an open field to die. She wasn't washed at her birth; she was naked, and her umbilical cord hadn't been cut off. (This kind of thing still happens today in many cultures in different ways. Many people just don't understand that every girl baby is destined to be a Princess.)

But just after they left her there, a True King came by on the road. He heard the crying newborn and went over into the field to find her. He decided that she should not die but live.

So he wrapped her in his cloak and took her into the next town. He found a good woman to wash the baby, nurse her, and raise her. The nurse very quickly learned to love the baby, as she was lively and warm-hearted. And she had the natural grace of a True Princess.

The King was obliged by his royal responsibilities to travel far away, but every year he sent the good woman silver coins, enough to pay the expenses of raising the girl.

Then after many years, as the King's own son the Prince had grown to adulthood, the King wanted to return to that town to see how the girl was doing. So he and the Prince traveled there to visit her. The King was amazed to see that she had become a young woman!

The King ordered new clothes for the girl. And not just any clothes; he commanded the finest tailor in the town to dress the girl like a princess: silk clothes, an embroidered jacket, fine shoes, a necklace, bracelets, rings, earrings, a nose ring, and a beautiful crown.

Then everyone saw that she was the most beautiful young woman of the town. Indeed, many said she was more beautiful than any girl they had ever seen, anywhere.

After some time spent getting to know her, the Prince made his decision. He asked her to be his Princess! She gladly accepted, for in the time they had spent together, she had grown to care for him deeply. They were betrothed according to the custom of that day. The Prince ordered more clothes for her and more jewelry, until she was the richest person in town. He also ordered the best food for her, made from only the finest flour and olive oil and fruits and vegetables.

At first, the Princess loved the Prince with her whole heart. She had never met anyone so kind and accepting, yet so strong and honest and pure. He seemed to have a kind of light shining from his eyes, and in his presence, nobody could tell a lie or say cruel things about anyone.

But then he had to be away on royal business, and while he was gone, other young princes started to come around, because the fame of her beauty had gone out far and wide. When they got to know her, they realized that she was also very wealthy. So even more of them came around.

When the Princess realized just how attractive she was, she trusted in her own wealth and beauty. This is a particularly dangerous kind of pride, for she forgot all that the Prince and his father, the King, had done for her—even saving her life—and started to believe that her beauty was due to her own efforts.

The Princess started giving herself to the other princes. And she started to spiral down into behavior that became more and more hideous.

By the time the Prince returned home, he found his Princess gone. But this Prince was a Prince of pursuing love. He was determined to search for her. (There is always a separation in these stories, a time of loneliness and testing and temptation.) The days stretched into weeks and then months, even years. At long last, the stories of the Princess' many lovers reached him. He couldn't believe it. So once he found where she was living, he asked her if the horrible stories were true.

And they were.

His heart was broken. Imagine how you would feel if your beloved wife or husband was not just unfaithful once with one person, but many times and with many people. It would be the worst feeling imaginable.

He confronted the Princess, not only heartbroken but furiously jealous. "How could you do these things? How could you forget all that I did for you? You took the wedding gifts I gave you, and you gave them to your lovers! You are worse than a prostitute, in your vaulted chamber with the huge bed! At least a prostitute gets paid for what she does, but you paid others to lie with you! And you took your children and sacrificed them in fire to idols! You who were saved as an infant, you put other infants to death! How could you do these things?!"

The fury of the Prince shocked the Princess. She had never seen him this way. She had never known righteous anger before. And when he finished, he looked at her with inexpressible sadness, saying, "We cannot live together as husband and wife anymore, for you have chosen your lovers. I am releasing you to them."

The Princess continued in her wickedness, and her life became more and more painful to her. Her lovers turned on her and cast her out. All of her jewelry and fine clothes were gone, because she had given them all away until there was nothing left.

She became tormented by the memory of what she had done... how she had failed the Prince... the horrible things she had done with the other men… and worst of all, the screams of the babies she had sacrificed in the fire. She feared she would be punished, and in her heart of hearts, she knew that she *should* be punished.

Finally, trembling, she set out to find the Prince. Pale and severely dressed, she threw herself at his feet and poured out her remorse.

The Prince said, "I forgive you. You have suffered enough. I can see that you have truly turned away from your past. I am going to re-establish the covenant I made with you in your youth. It is true that the memories of your shame shall always be with you. But I shall love you with an everlasting love, and you shall reign with me over my Kingdom."

But this story didn't end there. For the rest of it, you're just going to have to read the original. The author of this one is the Most High God Himself, and He is both Prince and King in the story. The Princess is His people.

He told this story through the prophet Ezekiel, at a time when the love of the people for Him had grown cold (chapter 16). He was trying to get through to them, trying to communicate just how much He loved them, with an intense, jealous, fiery love. He was saying that His heart was broken. He was feeling like a husband rejected by an incredibly unfaithful wife.

He loves each of us like that. His love is not some vague, philosophical idea. He loves us passionately, tenderly—always.

When I was a new Christian, I couldn't understand why there was so much horrific detail in this catalogue of the sins of Israel. Why was it necessary? Afterward I came to understand that it's because when God sees, He sees all there is: all of reality. And He does not flinch from it or cover it up.

But this story is, above all, about nations. It is especially about His nation, Israel, who He raised up and established. It's also about how He sees all nations.

In Ezekiel 16:46, He calls Samaria the older sister of the Princess, who lived with her daughters to the north of Israel; and He calls Sodom the younger sister, who lived with her daughters to the south.

In other words, the Most High sees nations as families of Princesses, more or less related.

When He speaks to the nations through His prophets, the pronoun used is always the feminine singular, "her" or "she." That's why this is not a story about "bad women." It's a story about all of us, women and men alike.

We also see families of nations, especially when it comes to languages. In Europe, we have the Latin family of languages (and therefore nations): the Slavic, the Germanic, the Scandinavian, the Finno-Ugric, etc. In Asia, there are the Sinitic languages, the ones related to the Chinese peoples (such as the Thai language, once thought to be related to the Turkic ones); and on and on.

The Lord sees the families of nations, and He also sees them the way He sees Israel: as the Princess each was created to be, but also as the Prostitute they have become.

For example, all the nations of Europe went to the House of the King and danced with the Prince; in other words, they were all Christianized, to a greater or lesser extent. And in some ways, just about every one of them has turned to other gods and is rejecting their Christian heritage, especially the laws. They have done just as Israel did in Ezekiel 18.

If we want to be effective in ministry in the nation to which He has called us, we must see her as He does. And this is very, very difficult to do, since most of us see only the one or the other. For example, we usually see the Princess in our own nation: we see her good points and minimize the bad ones. Here's a test: how do you react when someone criticizes your nation? Have you seen her Prostitute dimension? What about in yourself, whether you are a man or a woman? Do you see both the "Princess" and the "Prostitute" within?

Yes, it's difficult to see without Divine help. But if we ask, He will help us to see as He sees. And we can ask Him to see cities, regions, and peoples with His sight, as well as nations.

If we only see the Prostitute, the bad points of a nation, we will not have hope for her future, and we will not love her as God does. People pick up immediately on whether or not you love them; love is the ultimate cross-cultural communication.

But if we only see the Princess, we will not be able to intercede effectively for the nation. The most powerful intercessory prayers in the Bible are those of Moses in Exodus 32:31-34; of Ezra in Chapter 9; of Nehemiah in Chapter 9; and of Daniel in Chapter 9. These men see the sins of the nation and confess them to the Lord, and the Lord forgives. This is a far more powerful way of praying than just asking God to bless the nation. But to pray this way, we must see the horror and gravity of every sin, the way God does.

As we confess the sins of the Prostitute, we call out to the Princess! We remind her of her calling, her destiny. We appeal to her better side. We introduce her to her Prince. Music, dance, and the other arts are the best for this type of powerful, spiritual communication. Children are especially effective in these kinds of ministries.

The nations, like Cinderella in the first story, have forgotten their royal identity. They live under false names because they've forgotten where they have come from, and so don't know who they are, nor where they are going. Many of them had Cinderella names forced upon them by their colonizers, such as Argentina, named by the British because of the silver ("argent") they sought there. In many colonial situations, the colonizers were the nasty stepsisters or stepmother out to steal the inheritance, especially the mineral rights. Of course, there were those who thought of themselves as idealists as well, desiring to bring "the fruits of Western civilization" to these nations: not realizing that this is just another way of being a wicked stepmother. They forgot that all the nations have Princesses within, not just those of Western civilization. And so in their ignorance, they assumed their own culture was superior —the only true Princess—and they often forced others to speak a different language, outlawed certain indigenous practices, and tried to impose a different identity on the peoples.

Venezuela was named for Venice, because the Venetian people live in houses built out into the water, and the first Europeans who invaded Venezuela were reminded of the Italian city. Burkina Faso in West Africa was originally named Upper Volta by the French; after the indigenous people won their independence, they decided to change their name to Burkina Faso, which means "country of the upright." Christopher Columbus named America for a wealthy nobleman who sailed with him, Amerigo Vespucci. So the Americas have their names because of a fund-raising strategy!

Several years ago, a Tuareg named Ahmed came to attend one of our Discipleship Training Schools in Togo. A recent convert, he was encouraged by a missionary to travel all the way from Niger in his blue robe to get some grounding in his new faith. Listening to this message, he realized that his people had been given a Cinderella name by the Arabs who came to trade with them. "Tuareg" means "forgotten of God" in Arabic, and the traders called them that because they resisted conversion to Islam for so long. Indeed, they had been Christians in the early centuries and still wear the "cross of Agadez" around their necks, a stylized cross named for one of their principal cities in the Sahara.

So Ahmed returned to his people with a new message, which he broadcast many times over the radio: *"Tuareg" is not our true name, because we are not "forgotten of God"! It is a name imposed upon us. It does not describe our true identity, and we should no longer accept it. Let us take on a new name: "Kel Tamasek," the people who speak the language called Tamasek.*

This message was well received by his people, and it has opened a door for the Gospel, as Ahmed explains why he is convinced that they are not forgotten of God—because God the Father sent Jesus Christ so that they would have forgiveness of sins!

Many nations wonder about their true identity and are casting about for answers. They will find their true identity when they turn to the Lord. And He will reveal to them their new name, as He has promised to do for Israel when she accepts her final redemption (see Isaiah 62:2).

4

Caleb's Daughter and Othniel

Once upon a time, long ago and far away, a warrior prince strode through the land of his inheritance. Things were going well in the Kingdom and for him, but he had one concern: his youngest daughter was not married. And of course, true royalty does not think just of their own well-being, but also of the well-being of the future generations of the kingdom.

The Prince was pondering the fact that none of the young men had come forth to ask for the hand of this daughter in marriage. He suspected there were two reasons for this: for one thing, the girl was headstrong and very active. She would not be one to sit at home or to keep quiet when she disagreed about something. He loved these traits in her, and it saddened him that many young men saw strength and opinion in a woman as something undesirable.

Also, he realized that *he* could be intimidating the young men. He was old—much older than they—although still strong and vigorous, and his sight undimmed. He had led them through five years of warfare, winning battle after battle. He admitted to himself that at their age, he would have been reluctant to approach such a man also.

Then he hit on a plan. He called his young men around him and said, "One fortified city remains to be conquered in our lands. To the one who takes it, I will give my daughter Acsah as wife."

Othniel, the son of his brother Kenaz, immediately took up the challenge. He organized the attack, led it, and conquered the city.

Then Caleb blessed the marriage of his daughter with Othniel.

But Acsah had thought much about her inheritance. It had been one of the themes of their family talks around the campfires. She would often say to her father, "Tell me again about our inheritance, about how wonderful it will be."

And her father would tell the old story about him and the other eleven spies, one from each tribe, crossing the Jordan into the Promised Land.

Her favorite part was about the fertile soil, the green hills, the springs that watered the land, and especially the bunch of grapes that was so big and heavy that it had to be carried on a pole by two of the men. It sounded so different from the arid desert where she had spent most of her life (see Joshua 14:6-15).

So Acsah had decided when she was a little girl that she wanted a green farm with springs and grapevines. She persuaded Othniel to ask her father for land as her inheritance. She had only known a life of wandering until now, first in the desert and then during the last five years of warfare. She was so excited when her father told her he had already set aside land for her.

But when she and Othniel went to see the land, she saw that it was totally dry! Springs were located nearby, but not on their portion. They wouldn't be able to grow a thing without water. She said to her new husband, "Othniel! You must ask my father for those springs!" Othniel replied, "I asked him for the land, and that was hard enough. You ask him for the springs; you're his favorite daughter."

So Acsah rode her donkey back to her father's camp. She jumped off the donkey and ran up to her father. Caleb, knowing well when his daughter was coming to ask for something, said, "What do you want?"

"Father, give me a blessing! You have given me the dry land, but I need water. Give me the springs!"

So Caleb did.

Now, Caleb knew very well that the young couple would need water for that piece of land. Why didn't he just give them the springs when he gave them the land?

For the same reasons that the Lord doesn't give us everything He knows we need: first, He wants us to ask very specifically, and He also answers specifically. He wants us to use our minds to figure out exactly what we should be asking for.

Second, He wants us to keep coming back to him and communicating with him, for the sake of developing our relationship. Caleb knew that his daughter would come right back to see him as soon as she realized that there wasn't any water with that parcel of land.

Finally, Caleb blessed them mightily, giving them not only the upper springs but the lower springs also (see Joshua 15:15-19 and Judges 1:11-15). Then Othniel and Acsah put in their first crop, built their first little home, settled down and lived happily ever after.

Except that they didn't. Many years later, after the deaths of Joshua and the elders who had served with him, a generation arose who did not know the Lord or the mighty acts that He had done for Israel. They went after other gods, the gods of the peoples around them, and abandoned the Lord.

Then the Lord abandoned them. He allowed their enemies to plunder them, and since He no longer helped them in battle, they came under the power of evil rulers. One of the worst was the king of Mesopotamia. After eight years of his oppression, the people finally repented of the evil they had done and cried out to the Lord.

The Lord heard them and raised up a judge to deliver them. The man the Lord chose to deliver His people, the first of all the judges, was Othniel the son of Kenaz, Caleb's younger brother.

The Spirit of the Lord was upon him mightily, and Othniel led Israel out to war. The Lord gave him victory over the evil king, and the land had peace for forty years (see Judges 2:7-11).

So the true inheritance of Othniel and Acsah was not just a nice farm for themselves, but peace and prosperity for their entire nation. That's what happens when two people who have a call on their lives get married.

Which is also why the enemy of our souls contests so bitterly these kinds of marriages. Look at Loren and Darlene Cunningham, Bill and Vonette Bright, William and Catherine Booth, Samuel and Susanna Wesley, and many more examples from the history of the Church. The whole, in these cases, is greater than the sum of the parts. Marriages in the will of God are a key to the advancement of the Kingdom.

What are the lessons we can learn from this account of the relationship between Acsah and Othniel? After all, these lessons must be important, because their story is told twice in the Great Book.

First of all, Othniel was passive when it came to getting going in marriage, as are many young men and women today. He needed to be challenged, and Caleb found just the right one for him: not too big, but not too small either. Having this victory on his own was very important for Othniel, first because he was able to step out from Caleb's shadow, and second because the victory gave him the self-confidence he needed to be Acsah's husband.

So men and women of God, does the Othniel within you need to claim a victory before you marry?

What do I mean by a victory? I mean a challenge that's too big for you, one that forces you to press in to God and get to know Him in a new way. It could be an educational challenge, a professional one, or a ministry challenge. This won't be the case for everyone, of course: challenges come before marriage and after it, and they come to people who never marry, too. Press into God to discern, and He will be faithful to guide you!

Ask the Lord, and He will show you which fortified city is just your size... with His help.

I believe in this principle because I was called to live it out before I knew it existed. I was a new Christian, when just months after my conversion, I met the most beautiful preschool teacher in the world. It was springtime in Illinois; the lilacs were in bloom; the birds were singing…

I had never dated a Christian girl. It was totally different and totally wonderful. We prayed together every time we met, and our favorite "date" was being there every time the doors of our church opened (which was quite often, because in addition to the three weekly services, there were ten different outreach programs running that summer!).

Life was wonderful. However, I had a problem: after I received my B.A. from the University of Illinois, I didn't know what to do. I had wanted to attend graduate school in archeology, but my grades were not good enough to be accepted, as I had failed out of two universities before going into the Army and then being converted after I left. But that's another story…

So I was doing odd jobs that summer and praying about my future. But each time I prayed, the only thing that came to mind was "YWAM." I had heard a call to join this organization at my church, when a cousin of my pastor named David Boyd came through and shared about the mini-revival that was sweeping through the U.S. military in Germany. He said they needed more workers, and that they were asking for a one-year commitment.

I thought that this was wonderful, because I had prayed for the young guys in the U.S. Army. I had had a terrible time in the Army, and nobody in those three and a half years had shared the Gospel with me. The Army brass in Europe were open to YWAM teams coming in and living on the bases and running Christian coffeehouses precisely because the needs of the soldiers were so great: drug use, Satanism, and suicide were sapping the effectiveness of the Army. And at least a few of the upper echelon realized that the answers were spiritual. But I had just left the Army and had no desire to go back and live on an Army base. I especially had no desire to leave my Princess! Also, I had been separated from my family and from my country for two and a half years and simply did not want to leave again.

So I kept praying and kept receiving "YWAM," and I kept on resisting that call. Finally, one Sunday, I volunteered to drive a friend to three different churches so she could give her testimony about her outreach with YWAM. In the Pentecostal church, they sang the song, "Trust and obey, for there's no other way to be happy in Jesus than to trust and obey." Then we went to an evangelical church... and they sang the same song! I was distinctly uncomfortable. Last, we went to a rather liberal Protestant church... and they sang the same song! I knew it had been many a long year since that song had been sung in that church. So I bowed my head and told the Lord that I'd go.

When I told Cynthia what had happened but that I'd rather stay, she encouraged me to obey and to go to Germany for a year. She said we could stay in touch using the latest technology: cassette tapes! It took a long time for them to travel between Michigan— where she was working in a preschool— and Germany, where I ended up on the YWAM team on an Army base outside of Karlsruhe.

Those were long months, but as we each shared about what the Lord was doing in our lives, we realized that it was the same work!

And as I worked through my first small victories in the ministry, I gained the confidence to consider marriage. I proposed to Cynthia over Christmas vacation, and after another six months of separation and rapid spiritual growth, I returned to the USA, and we were married.

That year apart was very difficult emotionally, but it was the best preparation possible for our life together, and for our joint ministry. That was in 1972-3, and we were united and ministering together until her passing in 2012.

So don't be afraid to get your victory first, if that's what the Lord is calling you to do!

Othniel and Acsah were raised to think not just about their personal inheritance, but that of the nation. Indeed, this was the lesson of Caleb's life: that the destiny of one person is bound up with that of the nation. So when the time of God came for the deliverance of Israel, Othniel was open to the call of God. Acsah, the warrior's daughter, no doubt encouraged him.

Othniel rose to the challenge of judging the nation and leading it on to victory, just as he had risen to the much smaller challenge when he was a youth. A couple called to leadership, married in the will of God, can have not just a happy life but the chance to change a nation.

Our enemy knows this well, so he is ever trying to derail these kinds of marriages. Here are three of his most effective ploys:

One: Marriage is not an evangelism strategy. If you want to see someone converted, good! But don't marry them in hopes that they will. In the great majority of cases, a non-Christian loses all incentive to seek after God after marrying a Christian. If you really want the best for that non-Christian, don't marry them!

Two: Marriage is not a counseling strategy, either. How many times have we seen this scenario: a committed Christian starts ministering to a needy one; the needy person affirms how much they're being helped, which in turn encourages the strong person to go on helping; an emotional bond is formed, and they end up getting married. Bad idea! Any hope of a ministry can be destroyed by having to focus all one's time and energy on helping a needy spouse. If you want to counsel someone, fine; just don't marry them!

Three: Marriage should not override God-given calling. Any marriage between Christians has its basis in relationship with one another and with God; but for believers who have a specific call of God on their lives (such as to a specific ministry, job, community, or cause), a godly marriage must also be built on the foundation of a shared calling. In other words, if one partner is called to pastor a local church, the spouse must share that call. This is even more true of missionaries. One of the saddest sights in the Christian world is to see one spouse longing to go onto the mission field, while the other refuses to leave the home country. Knowing that the marriage is the priority, the one called to missions will refuse the call; however, the seeds of resentment of the stay-at-home spouse can too easily grow into bitterness.

However, the shared call to missions is general, not specific. In other words, if someone has a call to a specific people group, they do not always need to wait for a spouse with a call to that same people group! They can look for someone with a call to missions, but then both put their specific calls on the altar and seek God together about where to go as a couple.

The final question: what will your inheritance be? The one picked out for you by your parents? Grandparents? Friends? Culture? Inheritance is one of the most culturally bound concepts we have. In many countries, the cultural idea of inheritance is visible on the advertising billboards.

We see a happy little family with one or two children, a nice apartment or house, and a new car. The spirit of the nation is telling us that this is our inheritance, and the advertiser is telling us that we'll have it, if we just buy a certain soap powder, or cleaning fluid, or soft drink.

Of course, there's nothing wrong with a family, house, and car. They're biblical, even. But is that all you want from life?

So ask yourself: will you accept the inheritance that your culture, your family, even your church, has offered to you? Or is there more? What about the inheritance that the Lord has chosen for you? What about your nation? What about the nations?

Assignment: press in and ask God what His inheritance is for you. Hint: it's bigger than you think!

5

Abigail

Once upon a time, long ago and far away, a baby girl was born who was destined to be a Princess. Now her family didn't know that she would one day live in a palace at the right hand of the King; so the little girl didn't know it either.

Her family lived in a small village, a long voyage away from the capital city. The girl grew up with a strong sense of spiritual curiosity, and she asked her father if she could be educated in the things of God. In addition, she was a natural leader, the kind of girl who could organize all the children of the village into games and fun. But her family was rather poor and were concerned, as she approached the age for marriage, that they did not have enough money to furnish the dowry that would help ensure a good husband for their daughter.

One day, a rich man came to the village, as the news of this girl's beauty had gone all over the region. He was looking for a wife, but none of the families of his region would give their daughters to him in marriage, since he was a fool and had a mean temper besides.

The girl's parents didn't know any of this, so when he offered to give them a financial settlement in return for the hand of their daughter and described all the clothes and jewelry and servant girls she would have in his big house, they agreed. They thought they were doing the best thing for their daughter. And since she was a dutiful child, the girl agreed.

When the day of the wedding arrived, people were surprised that the man did not bring any of his family with him: just one man, whom he introduced as the foreman of his ranch. But since the prospective husband had invited the entire village to a huge marriage feast he'd paid for—a feast filled with lots of good food and wine—nobody asked questions.

The first couple years of her marriage passed like a whirlwind. The young woman lived in wealth on her husband, Nabal's, estate. She also had to learn how to manage the place. Her husband was a rancher with thousands of heads of livestock, so he had many men working for him. He also had orchards, vegetable gardens, workshops, and everything that goes into making a big household self-sufficient.

Reorganizing the work of the household servants, and the housing and feeding of all the ranch hands, took the young woman two full years. After all, she was still a teenager and had never even lived in such a big house with many servants, let alone tried to run such an operation.

But her natural talent for leadership served her well, as she was both diplomatic and quite strong. Her husband was happy with her taking on more and more responsibility around the place. He didn't get along well with people and didn't mind giving his young wife more and more to do.

However, after she had gotten the big place running smoothly, she started to realize just how mean a person her husband was.

He didn't have any friends and was too stingy to invite people to their house—although they probably wouldn't have come anyway, since he tended to get drunk and insult people. He would not allow her to go into town to make household purchases, insisting rather that she send for the merchants to come out to the ranch.

So her life became very lonely. The servant girls were not interesting company, and she had no more projects to work on. At this time in her life, she realized that her marriage had become a prison for her, and she was trapped for life. In that traditional culture, divorce was not an option.

So she decided to use her time to commune with God. As she consecrated three hours of her day to be alone with Him, His voice became more and more clear to her; and then she realized that He was leading her into being an intercessor for His Kingdom.

One day, during sheep-shearing time, a band of young men came riding down the trail to the ranch. They came up to Nabal and his men and greeted him in the following way: "Greetings on this day of prosperity! We are the ones who have guarded your herds and flocks this entire season, and it is due to our presence in the mountains that you lost not a one of your animals to wild beasts or to theft. So if you would like to bless us this day with some food, our master David would receive it with gratefulness."

Now this was a culturally appropriate greeting, and normally a wealthy man would be generous toward those who had helped him avoid costly losses. But Nabal answered them harshly: "Who are you, and who does David think he is? There are many servants running away from their masters these days! Why should I take the food and water that I have prepared for my men and give it to people whose origin I do not know?"

Now, to question someone's origins was a deadly insult in that culture (as it is in most other cultures, as well). Nabal might well have been referring to the story, still told in Jewish tradition, that David's parents were not married at the time of his birth. This would explain verse 5b of David's Psalm 51, "In sin did my mother conceive me…" It would also explain why Jesse did not bring David out when Samuel arrived in his house and asked to see all his sons. Jesse would have been ashamed of David's illegitimacy and might have assumed that Samuel would only want to see his legitimate sons.

David's men were angry at being shamed before all Nabal's men and rode off to tell David what had happened. David was having a bad week already. Not only was he having to keep on the move to escape being captured by Saul, he had just heard that Samuel had died. Samuel, the prophet of God, was the one who had anointed David to be King over Israel. This word of the Lord, which seemed so wonderful when David first heard it, and so possible when he was general over Israel's armies and leading them to victory after victory, now left a bitter taste in his mouth whenever he thought of it. And this week, his last remaining link with that word was gone, and he was having a hard time seeing how that prophecy could ever come to pass.

So when he heard from his men that on top of all this, the man known round about as "Worthless" had dared to mortally insult him and his men, anger welled up in him. David commanded his men, "Four hundred of you mount up and come with me; we are going to kill Nabal and all his men. Two hundred of you stay and guard the baggage." And David rode off at the head of the column.

Meanwhile, back at the ranch, one alert young man, who had done a Discipleship Training School, realized that his life was in danger. He also realized that Nabal was neither intelligent enough nor gracious enough to do anything about the situation, and that this group of unarmed ranchers had no chance at all against David's experienced warriors.

But he knew the one person who could save the household. So

he went to his mistress, Abigail, and said: "Today David sent messengers out of the wilderness to ask our master for a gift of food as they have guarded us all this past year; we lost not a one of the herd animals. They were like a wall for us both by night and by day. But our master answered them rudely, and they rode off in anger. Now, please consider what you should do, for we are in mortal danger. And our master is so worthless that nobody can speak to him."

Abigail instantly went into action. She called all the house servants to her and gave them detailed instructions to load up a string of donkeys with the best foodstuffs in the storage rooms: two hundred loaves of bread, big skins of wine, five dressed sheep, clusters of raisins, cakes of figs, and roasted grain. Then she sent the donkeys ahead of her toward the mountain where she knew she would meet David on his way to the ranch.

She ran to her own donkey and followed quickly, knowing that she had only a little time to try to stop David. David, meanwhile, was muttering under his breath as he rode down the mountain, saying, "I'm going to kill that Nabal, deader than dead, and I'm going to kill all his men with him. After all I did for him! He didn't lose a single animal. And he even insulted me! Just you wait; I'm going to kill him. He's going to be very, very dead."

Then he looked up and noticed a string of donkeys coming along the path. They were laden with food: some of the best food he'd seen in months. His men behind him saw the donkeys, too, and were exclaiming at the sight of the good home-cooked food.

And all of a sudden, David saw a striking young woman riding on a donkey, coming toward him. What was such a strong woman doing out here on the edge of the wilderness? As she approached, he could see that she was richly dressed with exquisite jewelry. She rode up to him, then slid off her donkey and bowed to the ground.

As David dismounted, she got up, came over to him, and fell at his feet. At that moment, a wave of the most powerful perfume David had ever smelled washed over him. The blend of aromas of spices and flowers reminded him of his time in the palace of King Saul. It almost made his head spin.

Then the lady began to speak. "On me alone, my lord, on me be the guilt. Please listen to me. Let not this worthless fellow—Nabal is his name, and indeed he is worthless—let him not bother you. [Nabal means fool in Hebrew.] Do not pay any attention to him. If only I had seen your young men, things would have been very different. Now the Lord is restraining you from bloodguilt and from saving yourself with your own hand. Please accept this present of food for your young men. Please forgive our wrongdoing. The Lord will certainly establish you as you are fighting His battles. The Lord will protect your life but not the lives of your enemies. The Lord will bless you powerfully and make you prince over Israel. So let there be no innocent bloodshed or taking vengeance in your own strength in the foundations of your Kingdom. And when the Lord has dealt well with you, remember me…"

David realized that this woman was not just beautiful, but strong and spiritually astute; and in his apostolic anointing, he recognized that she was also a prophetess, as she was bringing the Word of the Lord to him. "Blessed be the Lord God of Israel, who sent you this day to meet me!" he replied to her. "And blessed be you and your discernment, who have kept me this day from bloodguilt and from avenging myself by my own hand! For as surely as the Lord God of Israel lives, if you had not restrained me, Nabal and all his men would have been dead men by morning. Now, go in peace to your house. I have granted your petition."

And David rode off with the donkeys laden with food. Abigail went home to find that Nabal, in her absence, had ordered the servant girls to prepare a huge feast, and he was very drunk. So she didn't even try to talk to him until the morning light.

Then she went in and told him what had happened and how close he had come to death.

Following this news, he had a heart attack, and ten days later the Lord struck him, and he died. The news of the death of Nabal came to David, and he said, "Blessed be the Lord, who has avenged the mortal insult I received from Nabal, and who kept me back from wrongdoing. The Lord has returned the evil of Nabal back on his own head."

Then David sent some of his young men to bring Abigail to him as his wife. They arrived at the ranch house at Carmel, greeted her, and said that David had sent them to bring her back to him to be his wife. She gave the formal cultural reply and then jumped up and went with them, with her five servant girls. They were all packed and ready to go!

What is going on in this account? How did Abigail know that David would send for her to be his wife? How did she come up with such a convincing seven-point prophetic word for him in such a short time? She only had a few minutes to think of what she should say as she was riding toward the mountain on a donkey. How did she come to be so well- prepared?

How did she even know that David was the Lord's chosen one for kingship? Her husband obviously didn't, and none of the men of his household did. The villagers round about didn't, as they were trying to betray David to Saul (see I Samuel 24:1 and 26:1). How did Abigail know these things that were hidden from those around her?

Here is what I think happened. After Abigail realized that her marriage had become a prison, she turned to the Lord. Did loneliness and despair push her toward Him? Did a priest or an older woman of God point her in His direction? Did she remember childhood teachings from her parents? We don't know.

Perhaps one day she was listening to the well-worn argument about David's exploits and calling, with some saying that the rumor that Samuel had anointed him to be the future King was true, and with others saying that the House of Saul would rule over Israel for generations. That day, she decided to ask God how He saw David; she had learned to recognize His voice, He spoke to her daily, and she had learned that the way He saw people was usually very different than the way others saw them.

That day, as the Lord revealed that David was a man after His own heart, she understood that she was called to be an intercessor for David and for his kingship to be established over Israel (Amos 3:7). As she prayed day after day and sought after God intensely, she made the Lord her teacher. She looked forward to the time each day when the household was running smoothly and she could spend time in the presence of the Lord.

More and more, she understood principles of the Kingdom, and she became a powerful intercessor for the Kingdom. And in one of those times of prayer, the Lord whispered to her that she would have a role in the coming Kingdom next to David. So she said to David, "When the Lord has dealt well with you, remember me…" And David did remember and sent for her, and she was ready to go!

What are the lessons we can learn from the life of Abigail?

First, she was totally free of any cultural dregs of passivity. Hearing of the approaching danger, she immediately went into action and organized all the household servants into the rescue plan. This lady was ready to act in righteousness.

Second, this image in I Samuel 25 is the perfect portrait of an Intercessor. When Abigail learned that judgment was coming upon her household, she stood in the gap. She literally placed herself in that gap created by sin, identified with the sin, and asked for the judgment to be stayed. This is what a biblical intercessor does; it's what Moses did in Exodus 32:31-32. She could not be certain of David's reaction as she bowed before him; he was a man of violence, furious at Nabal. But she interceded for the life of her husband and his household.

Third, she was convinced of the principle that a kingdom cannot be built and last if there is a crack in the foundation. And the crack, in this case, was going to be David's reaction in fleshly violence, seeking revenge by his own hand and killing men who had done nothing worthy of death.

Now, David knew this principle already and had just passed this test with Saul in I Samuel 24. As Saul came into the cave where they were hiding, one of his men started prophesying that the Lord was delivering him into David's hand, and David should kill him. David knew the principle that he should not put out his hand against the Lord's anointed, and that it was not up to him to accomplish the word of the Lord to him through violence, but that he was to wait for the timing and the plan of the Lord.

Practical application: In the beginnings of any new ministry, the enemy often lays traps of unrighteous shortcuts. And he will inspire certain friends to prophesy that they are the right ways!

In my experience, these are often relational or financial. In other words, we can be tempted to violently cut off a relationship in starting a ministry, to break commitments, or to leave a group and slam the door, in order to be free to follow the Lord's calling.

The other temptation is to accept financing for the ministry that is not totally righteous. For example, a businessman who wanted to help the beginning of my ministry offered me the finder's fee for a house he was selling. In other words, if I signed a paper saying I had found the buyer, I would have received a fee worth many thousands of dollars.

The only problem was, I didn't find the buyer, so that would have been a lie. He urged me to accept, saying that it was a common practice. But I knew I had to refuse, even though that severely strained our relationship and he stopped supporting us (though he did come back some years later).

So don't be tempted to open a door to unrighteous "violence" in the beginning of your ministry. David passed this test with Saul but was going to fail it with Nabal. The Lord sent His intercessor with a prophetic warning that stopped him from this sin.

Abigail spoke with such prophetic authority because she had just passed the test, too! She could have said to herself, when hearing that David was coming to kill Nabal, "Praise the Lord! He's sending David to deliver me from this foolish husband! I'll just go visit Mother in town this afternoon, and tonight I'll come back as the heir of all Nabal's fortune! The Lord is using David to fulfill his promise of deliverance!" All Abigail had to do to be free from her prison was... nothing.

But her eyes were no longer on her prison walls. She had let her prison be transformed into a school where the Lord was her teacher, and His daily teaching was precious to her. Then, as she focused more and more on Him, the school was transformed into a temple, and the walls melted away as she fixed her eyes on Him.

The Lord had told her she would have a role with David in the Kingdom, but she knew that she couldn't try to bring about her own deliverance. She would wait and trust God, His plan, and His timing.

The principle is found in Psalm 105:19: The word of the Lord will test us. David had a word of the Lord—from Samuel, no less—that he would be king of Israel. Then everything fell apart, and he went from being Saul's favorite general to being pursued by a murderous Saul. Or take Abraham and Sarah, who instead of waiting for the promised son Isaac, took matters into their own hands and used Hagar to give them Ishmael. The temptation is when we know for certain that the Lord did indeed speak, and an opportunity for a violent shortcut comes up, and we want so badly to take it, having waited years for that word to come to pass.

The Kingdom principle, which Abigail saw so clearly, is that God's work must be done in God's way. *How* it comes to pass is much more important to the Lord than *when*. And He cares far more about preparing us than we do; we are always frustrated at the time it's taking to see forward progress. But the preparation is everything. Without the forty years in the desert, Moses could not have led Israel out of exile. Even Jesus waited thirty years to be ready for the beginning of His public ministry.

We read later that Abigail bore David a son in Hebron, so she reigned with him there.

Unfortunately, she must have died at a young age, as we hear nothing further about her. David needed her prophetic voice later on, but she was gone. Apostles need prophets to help them stay true to the ways of the Lord, and Abigail was that voice to David, at least in the early years. She might have saved David from some of his later mistakes, which cost him and the kingdom dearly.

Another practical application that arises from Abigail's story is this: There are many prisons. Marriage or singleness; sickness; depression; phobias or bitterness; lack of finances; family or neighbors; a job or joblessness; expectations of others; or religious traditions. What is yours?

Prisons are everywhere. We all live with constraints. We are all surrounded by walls of different types, heights, colors, and forms. The point is, what will we do with them? Will we focus on the walls, or on the Lord? Let the Lord transform your prison, first into a school, and then into a temple.

We can consider too that there is a type of leadership that is a wall around us. It's like David's men: invisible, but very effective. This type of leadership gives us a wall of spiritual protection that leaves us free to go about our work down in the valley. Practically, they can be our pastor or elders, our parents or grandparents, or the older generation of the organization in which we work. But because they are not down with us in the valley, we do not always understand that what they do is important—even critical.

We can be tempted to ingratitude, just as Nabal was. Then this puts a temptation before them to react in violence to the ingratitude, just as David did. This is a common human dynamic; it is often intergenerational and is found in families.

For instance, the younger generation wants the family inheritance in advance. They want the parents to sell off the family house or farm, so they can have their inheritance immediately and not have to wait. The parents don't want to leave the house where they've spent their lifetime together, so they react in violence to the younger generation, trying to cut them out of the inheritance.

This dynamic is often seen in organizations also, as the younger ones want to push the old leaders out of power and take over themselves. They don't appreciate the sacrifices it took to build the organization, or they don't understand the values and want to change them. The elders are tempted to react in violence, to push the younger ones out, or to force them back into a position of childish obedience to their elders, when God is growing them to be the next generation of elders themselves.

Two biblical imperatives are given to us to defuse these two time bombs: generous hospitality, and gratitude. They are not optional.

Gratitude is an expression of humility and reminds us that we receive from others, and we owe them love (Romans 13:8). It values the other person.

Hospitality is one of the New Testament qualifications for leadership, and one of the reasons is that it inspires gratitude. Hospitality touches us so profoundly because, at a very deep level, we remember Eden. We remember a perfect garden, a home, a place where we knew we were meant to be content and fulfilled forever. But then we had to leave it, and ever since, we have been wanderers in exile, trying to find our way back to our place. So many human endeavors—whether art, music, redecorating an apartment, or gardening—are efforts to re- create that perfect space. We are deeply dissatisfied because we know that this place is not our home, even when we are in the house in which we grew up and perhaps even spent our whole lives.

And especially when traveling, we are vulnerable to that basic, deep-down insecurity. So when we are offered hospitality, especially in a place that feels strange and different, the acceptance that it signifies is deeply healing. And when we are welcomed into someone's home, the impact is even deeper. Even though we know we are still wanderers in exile, hospitality reawakens the hope and longing of finding our way home again. As we are hospitable, we demonstrate the Lord's love, welcome, and acceptance.

Who was and is a wall to you and your ministry? Have you expressed your gratitude to them?

And seek out occasions to be hospitable; as you bless others, you will be blessed in return.

6

Mary, Martha, and Lazarus

Once upon a time, long ago and far away, two sisters and a brother were born to be royalty. As is often the case in these stories, they did not know they were royalty. Their parents died when they were young; the story does not tell us how. But they had been well off, owning a big house in the center of the village.

The older sister was a teenager at the time of their parents' death and very capable. So the family agreed that she should inherit the house and raise her two siblings, and the three children should continue to live in the house together.

As with most people in this traditional culture, they had a large extended family and benefited from much help and many visits. Their village was located near the capital city, so any time the family needed to go to the capital, they would drop by and encourage the three.

The siblings looked forward to the visits of one of the cousins in particular. He was single and worked as a carpenter to support His mother and siblings, as His father had also died when He was young. He was helping His mother to raise His own brothers. Perhaps because of this sensitivity, He was especially attentive to the young boy in the family. He came to take on the role of the elder brother, the masculine presence that the young boy had not had.

After this cousin turned thirty, however, everything changed. Strange stories were told about Him, of doves, voices from Heaven, and miracles. Many of these stories were difficult for His family to accept, but some remembered hints of things they had heard about His birth and His time in the Temple at the age of twelve.

Some began to say that He was the Promised One, the Messiah. His own brothers and sisters did not accept that, but the three cousins began to believe it more and more.

So Jesus would stop by their house with His disciples when going to or coming from Jerusalem. They would welcome Him there, and Martha, the elder sister, would organize a meal for them all. The times of fellowship in that house were amazing.

Then one day the young boy, Lazarus, became sick. The two sisters were not too worried because they knew that their cousin, Jesus, had a ministry of healing. And they knew exactly where He was that week, so they sent a message to Him: "Lord, the one whom you love is sick" (John 11:3).

This is one of the most beautiful prayers in the Bible—so brief and so filled with trust. But one way to hear it better is to listen to what is not being said. What two things do the sisters not say in this prayer?

One is that they don't ask Jesus to do anything: to come, to heal, to act. Why not? Certainly because they are so convinced that He will.

The other thing they don't mention is the name of their brother. Didn't Jesus love everyone? How would He know who they were talking about?

It seems that Jesus must have often expressed His love for Lazarus, because Lazarus needed to hear that. In any event, it was true, because John underlines in verse 5 that He did indeed love them.

What then did Jesus do when He heard this beautiful prayer? The same thing he often does for me when I pray a really, really good prayer: nothing. Nothing at all. He doesn't move; He doesn't act; He doesn't answer.

And the most difficult thing is, He doesn't explain. Our culture believes that explanations are a right. But in my experience, the Lord is an awfully lot less interested in explanations than we are. (Read the book of Job for an example. Job never received even part of an explanation for what happened to him!)

And the ultimate reason that the Lord does not give explanations? Because He gives Himself. If we use Him as a source of explanations, we show that the explanations are more important to us than He is.

And we turn toward the temptation of the Garden, the temptation to know… the oldest temptation in the world, the temptation to turn aside from obedience and turn toward the delicious fascination of knowing. Will we be satisfied with God Himself, even if no explanation is forthcoming?

We can imagine the sisters sitting next to the sickbed of their brother. They would have exhausted all their home remedies, then perhaps gone to the wise woman of the village to see if she had any better ideas. But nothing helped, and their brother got worse.

The sisters may have started counting, which is what I do to remind the Lord that He still has enough time to answer my prayer. "If He left immediately after He received our message, He could be here tomorrow before noon!" But no band of men could be seen walking up the dusty road. "If for some reason he had to wait until the next morning to start back here, He should arrive by nightfall." Perhaps they sent a village boy to the top of the hill to see if he could spot a band of men in the distance… but nobody came.

Then, as they sat in despair next to Lazarus… he died. We do not know when, but usually it's around 2 AM, when the body temperature drops to its lowest point.

What a shock for the sisters. Death is always a shock. We can think we are prepared, but we are not; we can never be. It's even more of a shock when unexpected, and it's worse still when it's a young person with their whole life still to unfold.

It's an even worse shock when the family knows Jesus and knows that He can heal. Perhaps they've even seen Him heal in other cases. When they are convinced of Jesus' love for them, then they think, *Of course He'll heal our loved one! Of course He will! He has no reason not to!*

But Jesus did not heal Lazarus. He arrived back at Bethany four days after the death.

Martha was told He had arrived and hurried out to meet Him. She was still in shock, and she said to Him, "Lord, if You had been here, my brother would not have died!"

We can almost hear the pain in her voice as she flung this reproach into His face like a slap. We know she was still in shock, because in a traditional culture, it is unthinkable to say something this direct to someone without the customary greetings and preparation. She should have asked Him about the trip, offered Him a seat in the shade and a drink of cold water, asked about the ministry week just past, asked if He'd had recent news of His mother and family or of the family carpentry business or of the doings in Nazareth.

These are the questions we would ask in French-speaking Switzerland before getting down to business. In some African cultures, seven to nine questions, or more, are asked. When I queried our Egyptian students how long they would spend in cultural preliminaries before getting serious, they answered, "An hour."

So we know that Martha was in shock. Still, she must have seen something in Jesus's eyes, because she said, "Even now, I know that whatever You ask from God, God will give You."

Jesus answers, "Your brother will rise again." Martha is not happy at all with this answer. She says, "I know that he'll rise again in the resurrection on the last day."

Martha has made the same mistake that many of us do. She thinks that the resurrection is just a future event, a doctrine. She's thinking, "I've known about that stuff all my life, the resurrection, sitting on clouds in white clothes, playing harps with choirs of angels. I know about that, but that doesn't help me today, the day when we are mourning my little brother, because You didn't show up!"

Then Jesus makes this astounding statement: "I AM the Resurrection, and the Life; whoever believes in Me, though he die, yet shall he live. And everyone who lives and believes in Me shall never die. Do you believe this?"

And Martha makes a beautiful confession of faith: "Yes, Lord; I believe that You are the Christ, the Son of God, who is coming into the world." But we will see in a moment that she still doesn't understand that the resurrection is not just a doctrine or a future event but a Person, a Person whose name is Jesus!

Martha goes and calls her sister Mary, who goes out, weeping, and confronts Jesus. She says, "Lord, if You had been here, my brother would not have died!"

The same phrase that Martha used, word for word, thrown into His face like a slap. No greeting, no offer of a seat or a cup of cold water, just the bitter reproach. Why was it the same phrase as the one her sister used, word for word?

We can imagine them as they would have sat next to the deathbed of their brother through the dark night of his passing. In the pain of their grief, they would have voiced their questions: "Why didn't Jesus come? What was He doing that was so important? He could have healed our brother! He healed so many! He healed people He didn't even know. Even foreigners! He said He loved our brother. What does it mean, when He said He loved him but doesn't come to heal him?"

And over and over and over again, they would have repeated to one another, "If only He had been here, our brother would not have died!"

We can identify with the sisters, since each of us has had that same cry in our hearts, if not from our lips. "Lord, if You had been here, this problem wouldn't have happened… this disaster wouldn't have taken place… this relationship wouldn't have gone wrong…"

Why is He, who says He is the Light come into the world, so often absent from our darkest nights? When Jesus saw Mary weeping and all the Jews weeping with her, He was deeply moved in His Spirit and greatly troubled. He asked, "Where have you laid him?" They said, "Lord, come and see," and showed Him the tomb where they had buried their brother.

Jesus wept. Why did He weep at this point? At least four theories have been advanced: The first is that—since we are only a few days away from the arrest of Jesus and His crucifixion—Jesus, in standing before the tomb of His young friend, has a sudden vision of His own coming death. In His humanity, He wept for His own imminent death and burial in a cold, dark tomb. Personally, I don't care for this theory, as it smacks somewhat of self-pity. It does not fit the One Who "set His face like flint" to go to Jerusalem.

The second is that He is weeping for Lazarus. But why would He weep for him, knowing that He was going to raise him from the dead in five minutes? Lazarus was feeling no pain.

A third possibility—and a more believable one—is that He was weeping for the Jews, the people of God who were just as helpless in the face of death as any pagans. The fear of death is indeed a powerful force in this world, much more than we imagine. After all, is not the materialism we see even in the Church a consequence of the unvoiced belief that we need to get it all and get it now, that we should live for the rewards of the present and not for Eternity?

The fear of death is a terrible thing and is certainly the source of more sicknesses, depressions, phobias and irrational behaviors than we know.

There is a fourth possibility that would explain why Jesus wept before the tomb of Lazarus. He has spent three years with His disciples at this point, is soon to leave them, but has a major problem: they have understood only half of the revelation concerning who He is. They're convinced of the first part, that His healings, deliverances and other miracles attest to the fact that He is the Sent One of God, the Promised One, the Messiah.

But they have not grasped the rest: that He is not the politico-military ruler coming to re-establish the Kingdom of David and Solomon through force; He is the Servant King who will give His life for His people, after being arrested, tortured, and crucified.

"And after three days in the tomb, He will rise from the dead, and after appearing to many will ascend to the right hand of the Father." He had told them all this many times, for two years, and they would nod their heads, but He could see they didn't get it.

This was serious, because the plan was that they remain in Jerusalem, gather together, and wait for the coming of the Holy Spirit to form them into the Church. If they all scattered back home to Galilee after the Crucifixion, then there would be no coming of the Spirit with tongues of fire, and therefore no Church. It was imperative that they realize that the Crucifixion was not the end!

Then comes the message from Mary and Martha, followed by

Jesus asking the Father: *do I go to heal Lazarus?* And the Father replied, "Let him die. Let him die, then go and raise him from the dead. Your disciples will see a resurrection; they will realize that I have authority over death, and they will remember that the next time they stand before a tomb… *Your* tomb."

Jesus would have thought about the implications of this word. What about Lazarus? He wouldn't feel anything. He would just seem to be asleep for those four days.

But what about Mary and Martha? Jesus would have realized that they would have a very painful four days, the worst of their adult lives. But He was so close to them, closer in some ways than His own brothers and sisters, closer than some of the twelve.

I propose that Jesus thought that He could trust them with something very precious in His sight: an unanswered prayer. But when He realized that they had not been able to wait for four days and trust Him to care for their brother, He wept.

Who can make us weep? Only the ones we've opened up to. The 56th Psalm indicates that the Lord keeps all our tears in a bottle, and He writes them down as well. Since I am a very literal person, I tend to think this means that somewhere in Heaven there is a huge cellar, because here in Switzerland, we keep our precious bottles in a dark, cool, still place. So there must be millions and millions of bottles up there, of different sizes, each with a name on its label. You have a bottle up there, and so do I… and some years, we graduate to a bigger bottle.

If our tears are precious to the Lord, our prayers must be even more so. I believe that the Lord remembers each one, even if we forget them. He takes every one and weighs it, and even if He doesn't answer, He doesn't throw it away. He keeps it, since He may decide to answer it later. And He watches to see if we will continue to take that prayer as seriously as He does, even if He doesn't answer it.

After preaching from this passage for many years, I had a revelation from Higher Up: When we pray, we are trusting the Lord; but when He doesn't answer, He is trusting us.

Has He trusted you with an unanswered prayer?

Then Jesus, deeply moved again, came to the tomb. It was a cave, and a stone had been rolled against it. Jesus said, "Take away the stone." Martha replied, "Lord, by this time there will be an odor, for he has been dead four days." Is Martha scoring a point here, in public? Reminding Jesus that He is not only late but four days late?

Jesus answered her, "Did I not tell you that if you believed, you would see the glory of God?" We don't know how He said this, or with what look in His eyes, but nobody dared argue with Him any more, not even Martha, the older sister who was so good at telling other people what to do.

Jesus lifted up His eyes and prayed to the Father and then cried out with a loud voice, "Lazarus, come forth!" And the dead man heard that word of authority, sat up on the stone bench where he had been laid, and staggered toward the place where he had heard that voice. He was still bound with the grave clothes. He couldn't see at first.

He would have heard many voices he recognized, some weeping, some crying out with fear, others calling the neighbors with joy. And then he heard one more voice he knew well, the voice that said, "Unbind him, and let him go."

It hit me only a few years ago that Lazarus could not have heard this command with his physical ears… he was dead! And I don't think that dead men can hear. To check out this idea, I asked a group of doctors at a YWAM staff retreat if a dead person can hear, and all four doctors said that couldn't happen. Four doctors agreeing about something—amazing!

This word of authority was so powerful that it pierced beyond the veil, into the place of the dead, and Lazarus heard it with the ears of the Spirit. It was so powerful that it called him from the grave into the light of day, from death back into life. It was a word of the resurrection power of God, confirming that life is so many times more powerful than death.

What are the lessons we can learn from the resurrection of Lazarus?

The first is this one: that no matter how impressive and intimidating death seems to be, life is more powerful! Messengers of the Good News must have a daily revelation of the resurrection power of Jesus; ministry can be defined as taking the life of Jesus into places where death reigns. If we have this daily revelation from Him, then we can proclaim His life, sing it, live it, and testify of it. Our relationships, our serving, our living, will all reflect His life.

And the bonds of death and the fear of death will start to weaken over the group we are called to serve. Conflicts will lessen in intensity; rejection will transform into acceptance; truth will penetrate more easily; and people will want to work together for the good of the community. We have seen this happen time and time again, all over the world.

Second, we need to see if our hope is in the Lord Himself, or in our idea of what God must do and when. Our ideas about how God should work, if they are not totally from Him, are constructions of our own minds and therefore idolatry. We may think we are too sophisticated to make idols of wood and stone and put our trust in them, but we are very good at building up theories about 'How God Should Work Here', and trusting in them.

The Lord, in His love for us, will simply allow these constructions to crumble under their own weight. Then when we see that "in these idols there is no salvation," He waits for us to turn back to Him and not just to our ideas about Him. Mary and Martha had not put their trust in Jesus; if they had done so, they would have held firm. Instead, they had put their trust in what they wanted Jesus to do, and when: their own plan for Jesus.

Third, we can learn more here about hope. Because all of us can be tempted to do just as Mary and Martha did when their prayer was not answered: to bury it, along with their hope, in a dark place, and then roll a stone across it.

Although, this reaction is understandable, it is dangerous. Hope is central to the Christian life; it is not just a pleasant, optional emotion, as I believed as a new Christian. Hope is linked in the Word with the following qualities: purity, patience, courage, joy, salvation, assurance, stability, and perseverance.

Hebrews 6:19 tells us that hope is a sure and steadfast anchor of the soul, piercing into the inner place beyond the veil. This means that if we start to lose hope, we start to lose our spiritual anchor, and this is one reason that so many believers are unstable. Hope is the link between the seen and the unseen, the actual and the potential, what we have now and what could be in the future.

Further, hope is the very ground of faith. One of the key definitions of faith is found in Hebrews 11:1, that faith is the firm assurance of that which we hope for. So if we lose hope, we cannot by definition have faith. If we no longer hope, we cannot have the assurance.

The enemy of our souls knows very well the power of hope, which is why he is always trying to push us toward despair. (The word comes from the French *désespoir,* the annulation of *espoir,* hope). So we have to be active in maintaining and increasing our hope.

Here also passivity will be a trap for us. Indeed, the Hebrews 6 passage (v. 18) tells us that we must "seize" the hope set before us. It's a very active word in the Greek.

How does this work practically? Happily, we don't lose hope all at once. We lose it in categories. We lose it in areas where we have buried it. In other words, tell me where you've stopped praying, and I'll tell you where you've lost hope. I've met people who no longer pray for their families, for their church, for marriage, for physical healing, for financial provision, for the future, for their nations. Many have left missions because of a loss of hope for financial support, or for resolution of conflict. They have tried to pray in those areas and their prayers have not been answered, so they've buried their prayers—and their hope—in a dark place in their soul and rolled a stone across it. The problem is that after it's buried for a time, it can start to give off an odor…

I picture hope as a flame in our soul. Sometimes it burns brightly; sometimes it flickers; sometimes it's almost extinguished.

But the Lord gives us three ways to have hope.

One is our confession: We are told by the same writer of the epistle to the Hebrews to "hold fast the confession of our hope" (10:23). In other words, our words can either en-courage, or dis-courage: the latter ending up in that *des-espoir*, despair, loss of hope.

Our conversation together is critically important in teams, in communities, in families. Some seem to think they have received the ministry of discouragement or negativity, but those are not from Heaven! Philippians 4:8 gives us good guidelines for our conversations as well as our thoughts. Teams can be, and have been, destroyed by one person whose confession is constantly negative. Let us speak things that will give hope to others!

Note to sensitive folks: Sometimes news media can destroy hope for our nation or for our economic future. Personally, I don't watch television news. I prefer radio or Internet sources, where the images are limited and I can have more control over what gets into my mind. We cannot subject ourselves to thrice- daily doses of bad news and then think we can have hope for the future.

The Apostle Paul wrote much about hope to the believers of Rome. Even though they were not under direct persecution at the time, we can imagine the oppression of that imperial city, where idolatry was so strong (as gods and goddesses from all over the known world were worshiped constantly). He told them that the Scriptures (in their case, the Old Testament) were a primary source of hope (Romans 15:4). So if you needed one more reason to read the Bible daily, here it is: it gives your hope a daily boost.

The third engine of hope is prayer. The Apostle prayed a mighty prayer for the Roman brothers and sisters in 15:13. I have prayed it for many different groups on all the continents over the past twenty-five years.

Here is what I propose: Bow your head, close your eyes, and ask the Holy Spirit of God to bring to your remembrance every prayer and hope that you have buried in that dark place of the soul. Wait a few moments in silence with Him. He is faithful and will remind you of categories in which you no longer pray, in which you have lost hope.

Then pray the prayer of the resurrection over them—"Lazarus, come forth!"—and ask the Lord to resurrect that flame of hope in your soul. Pray the prayer of Romans 15:13, and read the promise of hope in Jeremiah 29:11-14. Practice the discipline of hope; nourish that flame in your soul, and you will be anchored, steadfast, and unbothered by the winds and storms. And you will have the ground of faith, ready to be built upon.

7

Ruth

Once upon a time, long ago and far away, a girl was born who was destined to be a key part of God's plan for the nations. We know nothing of her birth, her family, or her childhood; we do know that at some point her family met another family: refugees from the land of Israel fleeing the famine there.

Elimelech and Naomi had taken their two sons to Moab to find food. After some years, Elimelech died there, but his two sons found Moabite wives and lived happily together. One of the wives was named Ruth; the other was named Orpah. But then the two sons died.

After that, Naomi heard that the famine in Israel had ended, so she decided to return home to Bethlehem. Her daughters-in-law went with her, but after a short distance, Naomi told them to go back to their mothers. "I am too old to have a husband and bear sons; and even if I did, could you wait for them to grow up and then marry them? No, please go home and find husbands for yourselves." They all wept together, and then Orpah kissed her mother-in-law goodbye and left her.

Naomi said to Ruth, "Look, your sister-in-law has left to go back to her people and her gods; follow her now." Ruth replied, "Do not urge me to leave you or turn back from following you; for where you go, I will go, and where you lodge, I will lodge. Your people shall be my people, and your God, my God. Where you die, I will die; and there I will be buried. Nothing but death shall part you and me."

This statement of Ruth's is one of the most beautiful person- to-person commitments in the history of literature and is often used in marriage ceremonies today. It is also a powerful summary of the ultimate missionary calling: to completely adopt a different culture for love of the people. Most importantly, it clearly signifies Ruth's conversion to the Lord God of Israel; she is not only leaving her family and her nation, but also her gods.

As Naomi and Ruth arrive back in Bethlehem, they are warmly welcomed by the women of the city; and the story of Naomi's losses and Ruth's commitment to her is soon known by everyone. But their immediate need is food, and Ruth knows that she can go out and glean in the fields behind the harvesters. So she asks permission of Naomi, who releases her to go ahead.

The Lord leads Ruth to the fields of Boaz, who is not present when she starts work early in the day. When he returns and hears that she is the Moabite who returned with Naomi, he gives orders to his servants to let her be and tells Ruth how to proceed with her gleaning in safety.

He honors her commitment to Naomi and also her coming to the Lord: "May the Lord reward your work, and your wages be full from the Lord, the God of Israel, under whose wings you have come to seek refuge." Then he shares his roasted grain with Ruth at the mealtime and makes sure she has enough left over to take home to Naomi.

When Naomi sees how much grain Ruth has brought home, she asks, "Where did you glean today?" Ruth tells her that she was in the fields of Boaz. Naomi immediately recognizes the leading of the Lord in their circumstances. And Ruth says, "Furthermore, he said to me, 'You should stay close to my servants until they have finished all my harvest.'"

After the end of the harvest, Naomi tells Ruth, "Wash and anoint yourself, put on your best clothes, and go to Boaz tonight at the threshing floor. When he lies down, go and uncover his feet and lie down there; then he will tell you what to do, for he is our kinsman-redeemer." Ruth obeys Naomi, as she has at every point since arriving in Bethlehem.

In the middle of the night, Boaz woke up and was startled to find a young woman at his feet. Realizing immediately that by this gesture of submission, she was offering herself to him as a wife, he says, "May you be blessed of the Lord, my daughter. You have shown your last kindness to be better than the first by not going after young men, whether poor or rich. Now do not fear. I will do for you whatever you ask, for all my people in the city know that you are a woman of excellence."

Boaz went to the city gates the next morning and performed the
ceremony of the kinsman redeemer, publicly taking Ruth as his
wife. Then all the people in the court and the elders blessed Ruth
and the household of Boaz.

Soon afterward, Ruth bore a son, and Naomi became his nurse.
His name was Obed, and he had a son named Jesse. And Jesse
was the father of David the King. So Ruth, the foreign woman,
was part of the lineage of Jesus the Messiah, Lord of the nations.

Ruth is a woman of amazing faith, as she undertook a journey
similar to that of Abraham. To leave her family, her culture, and
her gods and go to another nation was a huge step. To say that
she stepped into an uncertain future is to put it mildly. How is it
that she had so much faith? I believe that her faith grew out of
her courageous love for Naomi, and then strengthened as she
walked in detailed obedience to her mother-in-law, to Boaz, and
ultimately to the Lord God of Israel.

Let's step back and think seriously about faith. We're not talking
in this chapter about "the faith," the body of beliefs that united
the early Church. We are talking about faith as authority, and
how to increase our level of it.

Faith is central in our Christian walk. We are saved by faith; we
have righteousness by faith; we have wisdom by faith; and we
receive the promises of God by faith. By faith we triumph over

the world and over the devil. We prophesy by faith. We receive healing and the ministry of healing by faith.

And Jesus said that if we have even a small bit of faith, we can move mountains.

Amazing! As we continue in our walk with the Lord, we come across mountains: huge obstacles that loom up in our path and prevent us from going farther. What are your mountains right now? They can be financial, relational, work-related, or church-related. They can loom up in any area. Our nations often have mountains before them. What a privilege to be able to speak to any of these mountains and move the mountains aside!

And of course, we are all called to live by faith: to live our relationships, our finances, our families, all by faith. But the best reason for wanting more faith is that faith pleases God. Even if faith did nothing for us, we would want more faith in order to please our Lord.

When I was a young Christian, I was convinced of my need for more faith. Converted not long before my twenty-fourth birthday, I knew I had wasted years and needed to catch up on my level of faith. So I started to read every book and listen to every message I could find on the subject of faith.

But when I realized the principle of the "law of faith," I was shocked. This is the response of the Lord: when we pray, He says, "Let it be done to you according to your faith." Someone said, "The Lord hears prayer, but He answers faith." I thought to myself, "Oh no! I don't want an answer according to my faith! I want an answer according to Billy Graham's faith!" But no, we will always be answered according to our own faith level.

I found three theories on faith which were unhelpful. They weren't wrong, but they were incomplete and often led to misunderstanding.

The first was that faith is a gift of God (Romans 12:3). Now this is certainly true but not helpful, because everything is a gift of God—including life itself—and any blessing of God is unconditional. Also, when people said that faith is a gift of God, they tended to leave the impression that God had decided to give a lot of faith to some, such as Loren Cunningham, and not to others, who were standing behind the door when faith was passed out, such as myself! I decided that since faith was so central to the Christian life, the Lord wanted all of us to have more, and there must be a condition to receive more.

The second answer was that faith comes by hearing, which is also certainly true in part. But faith cannot come only by hearing; Jesus stated very clearly that just listening to His words was not enough.

In the parable of the man who built his house upon the rock and the other one who built his house upon the sand, most Christians will tell you that the problem of the guy who built his house upon the sand was that he didn't listen to Jesus. But that's not what Jesus said! They both listened to him; the one who built his house upon the sand didn't do what Jesus said. He makes clear that listening to Him and not obeying is not only useless but dangerous.

Most of us are from subcultures that are enamored of hearing. We think that if we listen to biblical teaching, we will become more mature. Many churches, when looking for a pastor, seek a New Testament expositor or a profound Bible teacher. All well and good, but those ministries by themselves will not lead to maturity in the church.

The New Testament is clear on this point: just listening to the truth will not necessarily help us (see Hebrews 4:2, Luke 8:21, Matthew 7:24-6, James 1:22-24). Those responsible for Christian groups should be leading them into doing the Word, not just listening to it or studying it.

If faith came only through hearing the Word, you could set up a continuous-loop recording of the Bible, and anyone who listened to it for eight hours a day, five days a week, for twelve weeks would come out a giant of faith. But nobody does that, because deep down inside we know very well that just listening is not enough.

The third traditional theory is not even biblical, and that is to pray for faith. We often hear when a team is going out on a missions trip, "Let's pray for them to have faith!" Nice idea, but we see that kind of prayer nowhere in the Bible.

Now, the Apostle Paul prays wonderful prayers for his young churches, in which he asks that they be given strength, wisdom, hope, love, and many other things. But he never prays that they might have increased faith. Since he well knew how crucial faith was for them, he certainly would have added faith to his prayer lists… if indeed faith came through prayer.

What, then, is the engine of faith? After ten years of seeking the answer, I was getting more and more frustrated. The French Ministries of YWAM were growing and developing with my leadership, and the Lausanne base as well; I could see evidence of my growing faith all around me, but I had no idea how or why it was growing! So I could not teach the others around me how to have more faith.

Then I was stopped in my tracks one day while reading Luke 17. In verse 5, the Twelve ask Him, "Lord, increase our faith!" Then Jesus gives an answer that is seemingly very strange: "If you had faith like a grain of mustard seed, you could say to this mulberry tree, 'Be uprooted and planted in the sea,' and it would obey you."

Now, I am a gardener, and while it would be useful to be able to move trees around my garden by faith, it wouldn't be helpful at all to uproot a fruit tree and plant it in the ocean! Besides, for once the Twelve ask the right question, in contrast to some of the other ones they asked (such as, "Can we call down fire on this Samaritan village?" "Who will be the greatest in the coming Kingdom?" "Can we have the best seats at Your table?").

So why did Jesus give such a cryptic answer about mulberry trees, when the Twelve had presented Him with a teachable moment, when He could have communicated something very important? In my opinion, He did answer their crucial question, especially in the verses that follow.

The problem is, many Bibles make separate paragraphs of these verses, giving the impression that Jesus's answer stopped with verse 6. That shows that many Bible translators and editors have more knowledge of linguistics than faith. To paraphrase verses 7 through 10: "Do you want more faith? Then do what your Master tells you to do! Obey him! When you are hungry... obey him! When you are tired of the long obedience and want to rest... keep on obeying! When others have left and you are alone out in the field... keep on doing what He said to do! When you do all that He commanded you, your faith will increase!" In other words, the engine of faith is... obedience!

This principle is also clear in the account of the healing of the centurions' servant (see Matthew 8:5-13). When Jesus arrives in Capernaum, the centurion asks Him to heal his paralyzed servant. Jesus agrees, offering to come to his house. But the centurion protests that this is not necessary, saying, "Only say the word, and my servant will be healed. For I too am a man under authority with soldiers under me. I say to the one, 'Go,' and he goes, and to the other 'Come,' and he comes, and to my servant, 'Do this,' and he does it.'"

When Jesus heard this, He marveled and said, "With no one in Israel have I found such faith!" Jesus then says, "Go; let it be done for you as you have believed." And the servant was healed in that moment. Jesus didn't have to go to him; He didn't even pray for him! The faith of the centurion had healed him.

Now, Jesus did not marvel at much. But this centurion's faith astounded Him. Why did the centurion have such faith? Because as an officer in the Roman army, he lived and breathed authority every hour of every day. This military organization demanded ongoing accountability and instant obedience, and the punishment for disobedience was death. Authority was not just a religious idea for him but his way of life; if he ever lost authority over his men, many could lose their lives in battle.

Luke tells us (7:4-5) that the centurion was not only under the authority of the Roman high command but under the authority of God. He was the one who had paid for the construction of the synagogue in Capernaum, and the reason he didn't want Jesus to come into his house to heal his servant was that he knew very well that Jesus would get into trouble for doing so. The Pharisees, who were in charge all around the district of Galilee, would not tolerate a Jew entering the house of a Gentile.

The centurion had a profound understanding of authority because he was under the authority of God Himself. As a Gentile convert, he would have sat under the teaching of the

Pharisees about the coming Messiah. Then when he heard of the debate surrounding Jesus of Nazareth (over whether He was the Messiah or not) the centurion realized that He had to be! Because anyone having the authority to do what Jesus was doing—calming the storm, feeding the multitudes, healing the sick, casting out demons—had to be under the authority of God. So he recognized that Jesus was also under authority, and this is why he said, "I, too, am under authority..." And he therefore knew that Jesus had the authority to heal a helpless case at a distance.

The Pharisees missed the Messiah because they were applying their religious criteria: the Messiah doesn't come from Nazareth... He would never heal on a Sabbath... He would not eat and drink with sinners... and on and on. The centurion recognized Him, because he understood the principles of authority; and he knew that the authority Jesus was manifesting could only be there if Jesus had been sent by God Himself.

So the question we must ask is not, "How much faith do I want?" but rather, "Just how much do I want to be under authority?" All the men and women of faith I have learned of lived lives of detailed obedience.

Kathryn Kuhlmann was the greatest healing evangelist in America in the 1970s; she had more healings documented by hospitals than anybody else, books full of them. She held meetings every Sunday afternoon in a small auditorium in Los Angeles, and people would stand in line for hours in the sun for a chance to get in. Someone asked her once, "Miss Kuhlmann, why don't you rent the larger auditorium just a couple blocks away? That way sick people won't have to stand in line for hours, and more people will hear the Gospel every Sunday." She immediately answered, "I dare not. I dare not, because the Lord has told me to use this auditorium."

This answer was incredible to me. I wouldn't even have hesitated to move the meetings. People waiting in line? A bigger place nearby? Let's go! But for Kathryn Kuhlmann, the place was part of her detailed obedience. And so she had faith for healing beyond that of any of her contemporaries.

If we hear the voice of the Lord and obey, we will have the faith to do what He is calling us to. For example, I know people who have heard from the Lord that they are to go and pray in every country in the world. They have received the faith to be able to do that, because it is their obedience. I haven't heard that from the Lord, so I'm not trying to visit all the countries I can; it is not my obedience. Therefore I don't have the faith for that, because I don't need it. When the Lord does tell me to go to some nation to minister, I find that as I obey Him, I have the faith for that trip: for the finances for the plane ticket, for the visa, for protection on the way, for travel mercies, etc. I have obeyed His commandment to "go," and I have the faith to do that whenever He says to.

This principle also applies in evangelism. Why is it so difficult for people to come to the Lord? Kierkegaard answered it this way: "It is so difficult to believe because it is so difficult to obey." Sometimes when we come back from trying to witness to resistant people, we will say, "They didn't believe the Gospel." But Paul says three times in the New Testament, "They didn't obey the Gospel."

Jesus said it this way in John 7:17: "If anyone's will is to do God's will, he will know whether the teaching is from God or whether I am speaking on My own authority." This explains why there's such confusion in the media and elsewhere about who Jesus is, and why we read such strange articles every Easter about The True Jesus. The different opinions of Him include that He was the first socialist, an incarnation of Vishnu, a Jewish rebel politician, an extraterrestrial, a student of Hindu thought in India during the ten years before His public ministry, etc., etc.

Why is it so hard to know who Jesus really is? Why can't we accept that He is the Sent One of the Father? Often, it's because we don't want to do the Father's will. We can't come to faith because we don't want to obey. (Of course, we are not saved by our obedience, but we have to at least want to have our heart inclined to obey God in order to be saved.) George MacDonald says it this way: "What in the heart we call faith, in the will we call obedience."

Obedience increases our faith, but the opposite is also true. Disobedience decreases it. This truth is expressed almost mathematically in Hebrews 3:18-19. The writer first says the reason that Israel could not enter the promised land was disobedience; then in the next verse, he says it was unbelief. The inference is clear: disobedience can lead to unbelief.

When I understood this principle, it cleared up a question I'd been holding for years. Early in my YWAM experience, I was on a team with a young lady older than me, with years more of walking with God. She was an intercessor, worship leader, could lead Bible studies, and witnessed intensely. I learned much from her. But then she started to question the wisdom of our leaders; then she questioned the Bible; and finally, she started asking if God was real. I was thrown by these questions. Could someone know the Lord so well and then begin to doubt? Could this happen to me? I was destabilized.

Then when I understood the above principle that disobedience leads irresistibly to unbelief, I realized what had happened. My teammate had started an intense relationship with an unconverted guy, persisting in the relationship against the counsel of her YWAM leaders, her pastor, and the local leadership. And as she persevered in this relationship, she lost her faith. Disobedience brought on unbelief.

As we share our faith with others, we often meet someone who says, "Oh, I used to believe all that stuff you're talking about. I used to go to church and witness. I even went on missions trips!

But I don't believe any of that anymore." If you pursue the conversation, you will find that the person began to lose their faith when they came to a crossroads of choice and decided to disobey God in a key area. They didn't just lose their faith; faith doesn't get lost like that. They chose disobedience, which inevitably results in unbelief.

It's not possible to lose your faith! Faith is not like a cell phone: "Where did I leave it? In my room? In the kitchen?" No, faith resides at such a deep level in our spirits that it cannot even be attacked. We cannot lose it, but we can disobey it away.

But the good news is, getting more faith is simple! Not always easy, but simple. Would you like to experience effortless righteousness? Be able to pray for concrete situations and see real results? Move mountains? Then just do the next thing God tells you to do.

How do we know what that is? First, read the Bible daily, since most of His will for us is revealed there. Second, ask Him in the place of prayer if He has a specific task for us for that day. Bake something for the neighbors? Encourage a friend? Pray for someone in need? Then just do whatever He brings to mind.

We must constantly hone our discernment of the voice of the Lord, to know exactly what He is saying instead of picking up only confused intuitions, unsure that we are indeed hearing God or whether we are just hearing our own thoughts. We sharpen our discernment by actually doing what the Lord said to do. Obedience to the word of the Lord prepares us to hear even better the next time. When we hear and do not do what He says, we often get more and more confused and end up by not hearing anything more, and in certain cases not wanting to listen either, for fear of what we might hear Him saying to do.

Faith is the very authority of God; in His wonderful economy, He shares it with those who walk ever closer with Him in the long obedience.

There's an important distinction to make here, between a faith crisis and "losing faith." In Christian circles, we often mistakenly think that someone who has doubts, who is asking questions, or who goes through a "dark night of the soul," is losing their faith. We think, "This is happening because they're sinning. If they would just confess whatever secret sin they are holding onto, repent, and turn back to God, their doubts and struggles will disappear, and they will be filled with a renewed awareness of the presence of God!" Sometimes, we even confront people who are struggling in this way, just like Job's "friends," insisting that their pain is their own fault.

But this is not true. In fact, dark nights of the soul are something that come to the very strongest of Christians. One third of the Psalms lament the absence of the feeling of God's presence; we see in the writings of Mother Theresa, or St. John of the Cross, or other giants of the faith, that God withdrew the sensation of His presence from them for stretches of time. Many people experience this. For strong believers, it can be a frightening and painful experience, and it is made worse by well-meaning Christians who want to "fix" it: *have you repented? Have you tried reading your Bible more? If you just pray…*

When my wife Cynthia was sick but we didn't know that she was dying, the Lord asked me this: "Would you still follow Me if I never answered any of your prayers again?" And I immediately responded: "Of course I would continue with You, Lord. I don't follow You because You answer my prayers." And He did not answer my prayers for her healing: nor the prayers of the many thousands (literally) of others who were praying for her around the world.

If this is where you are, I want to encourage you: you are not losing your faith. Faith is a growing deposit, located so deeply in the spirit that we cannot feel it, and it cannot be attacked by the enemy of our souls. When a faith crisis comes, a dark night of the soul, we can know that this, too, is not too much for God to handle. He is still the Author and Finisher of our faith! The Lord allows dark nights of the soul because they serve a crucial function in His work of sanctification: they purify our faith, even as we lose our ability to sense His presence. The Lord wants us to worship Him alone, not the blessings He gives us, not our ministries, and not even the heavenly feeling of His presence. The commandment "you shall have no other gods before Me" contains several levels of meaning we have yet to comprehend. But take heart: the Lord has not left you; He has only withdrawn from your perception of His presence. He does this for all of us, lest the feeling become more important to us than the Lord Himself. No matter what you feel, your faith is still there, unaffected by what you are going through. You have not lost your faith!

A faith crisis, then, is allowed by the Lord for our testing and growth, not as a result of some undiscovered sin. It cannot be avoided or fixed by praying and reading the Bible; it must be experienced. But losing faith, as described initially in this chapter, is a direct result of disobedience. And we usually know what it is we're refusing to give up.

Distinguishing between hope and faith is not always easy, and when we mix them up, we can get into trouble. Here's the principle: We can feel hope, but we can't feel faith.

In Loren Cunningham's first book, *"Is that Really You, God?"*, the story is told of two girls witnessing outside a village on a Caribbean island. They are telling an old man about Jesus, His ministry on earth, dying for us on the Cross, and so on. The old man asked, "Can Jesus still heal?" The girls replied, "Of course He still heals." Then the old man said, "Then I'd like Him to heal my hand; I haven't been able to move it for the past thirty years." He held up a withered hand that was literally skin and bones, no muscle left on it at all. Trapped by their testimony, the girls bowed their heads, and one began to pray hesitantly for healing. Suddenly the old man started shouting, "It moved! My hand can move!" And he ran off toward the village, shouting, "Come and see! Jesus healed my hand!" Whereupon the girl who was praying for him fainted, right there in the road. She had not felt her faith growing, but due to her repeated steps of obedience that summer, it had. And when she prayed, the Lord answered, according to her faith.

Another story is told, this time about an American evangelist who is having wonderful meetings. Every night people are getting saved and healed. One night, after a particularly encouraging meeting, he's returning to the hotel where he's being housed, thanking the Lord for the good fruit he's seeing. Seeing the big swimming pool in the hotel courtyard, he says, "I'm so full of faith, I think I could walk on water!" He stepped out onto the surface of the pool… and went all the way into the water.

On his way down to the bottom, he prayed, "Lord, why couldn't I walk on the water?" And the Lord answered, "Because *you* said you could walk on the water. I didn't." So the evangelist didn't have faith for walking on the water because his step was not in obedience to the word of the Lord. Peter could walk on the water *because the Lord told him to.*

In this sense, faith does indeed come by hearing the Word of the Lord, as we then do what the Lord has told us to.

Often we will hear a testimony in a meeting, and the leader will say, "Didn't that testimony increase your faith?" I always want to stand up and say, "No, it didn't! It increased our hope!" Because, as we saw in the previous chapter, testimony is one factor that increases hope. And since hope is situated in the soul (Hebrews 6:19), when it increases, we can feel it.

Contrariwise, when we start to lose hope, we can feel it; and we all know that feeling. The danger is that when we feel the hope surge within us, we can start to pray and nothing happens. Then we start to lose hope, and finally we bury it in a dark place.

Part of the problem is praying for a situation without that word of the Lord. This is sometimes the case in praying for healing. Before praying, we should ask the Lord how He wants us to pray. Does He want healing for this person in this moment? We need to know, or we may not be praying in obedience and therefore will lack faith.

Faith lies deeper than hope. Some would say it is situated in the spirit. So we cannot feel faith. We do know that faith is the firm assurance of what we hope for (Hebrews 11:1). We start to pray in hope, and we can feel that hope. But praying in faith is not the same as praying in hope.

When is hope transformed into that firm assurance which is faith? When the word of the Lord comes! When He speaks and says, "Now I will do this thing!" It was when Deborah said, "This is the day… !" (Judges 4:14) that Barak and all Israel had the faith that the Lord would do a miracle of deliverance. So to obtain hope, we read the Bible, pray, and concentrate on positive testimony. To get more faith, we listen to the Lord and do what He says, and as our obedience increases and becomes a way of life, our faith grows strong and sure.

But what is the engine of obedience? Is it all about gritting our teeth and making right choices? No, it's easier than that. See the next chapter…

8

Mary and the Alabaster Jar

Let's go back to Bethany. Remember, the village where Lazarus was just raised from the dead by Jesus? Jesus is back there, and if we go to the village and look into the window of the house of Simon the leper, we can see young Lazarus… and Jesus.

The window is the passage found at the beginning of the twelfth chapter of the Gospel of John. What can be going on in the mind of the young man who was dead… and then was called back into life? We don't know, but we can be sure he was looking at Jesus.

Martha is there, serving the dinner. Of course! What else would she be doing? That's how she expresses her love: feeding and organizing people.

Then Mary arrives. She's carrying an alabaster jar, one large enough to hold a pound of perfume. She pours it onto the head and feet of Jesus, wiping His feet with her hair. The whole house is filled with the aroma of what is obviously a very expensive perfume.

Judas, the disciple who would later betray Him, got angry and said, "Why wasn't this ointment sold for three hundred denarii to feed the poor?" He said this not out of any concern for the poor, but because he had charge of the team finances and used to steal from the common purse. And the other disciples started to scold her.

Jesus said to them (from the parallel passage in Mark 14:1-9): "Leave her alone. Why do you trouble her? She has done a beautiful thing to Me. For you always have the poor with you, and whenever you want, you can do good for them. But you will not always have Me. She has done what she could; she has anointed My body beforehand for burial. And truly, I say to you, wherever the Gospel is proclaimed in the whole world, what she has done will be told of in memory of her."

What an amazing statement. Jesus understood the message that Mary was giving Him, an unspoken, feminine message that the disciples understood not at all. And this message had to do with preaching the Gospel in the whole world, with missions! What was her message, which is crucial to missions and therefore to all of us?

To begin to understand, we must realize that the message cost Mary; it was an expensive gift. First was the financial cost. Judas immediately realized the cost of the perfume, being one of those people who know the price of everything and the value of nothing. It was the equivalent of a worker's annual wage. Of course, even today, a pound of high-end Parisian perfume would cost at least a year's salary.

Where did they get the cash to buy such a gift? Did they use their life savings? Or did they sell their house? Because they are not hosting this dinner in their own house; for the first time we see them in the house of a neighbor.

Or was the money the dowry they had saved so that Mary could be assured of a husband from an upper-class family? Did Mary literally pour all her future hope onto the feet of Jesus, all her hope of marriage and family? We don't know; the text is silent on this point.

All we know is that it was a costly gift. It cost in another way also. Mary came into that room full of men, whom she would have known her whole life, not as the youngest daughter of the wealthy family who owned the big house in the center of the village, but as a slave. Because in that culture, as in many parts of the East still today, the head is holy, and the feet are unclean. Even a Hebrew slave could not be asked to wash anybody's feet; only a foreign slave could be required to do so.

So the personal cost to Mary must have been huge, unimaginable to us today. She laid down at the feet of Jesus not only what she had—the finances—but who she was: the identity she had carried before her friends, family, and neighbors all her life. And possibly, if she had used her dowry money, it was her entire future as well, the hope of having a good husband and a family.

What was she saying to Jesus through this costly gift? I believe there are four messages here, at least. First, I believe that Mary, Martha, and Lazarus had agreed on this gift to say thank you to Jesus. This may well have been the first chance they had to publicly thank Him. After the resurrection of Lazarus, the text tells us (John 11:53-54) that Jesus was in imminent danger of arrest and had to withdraw into outlying areas. He probably left immediately after the resurrection, before the three were free of all the people wanting to see Lazarus alive again and rejoice with his sisters.

After the friends had left, then the family members, the three would have finally had some time together. That's when they would have realized that in all the commotion, they hadn't thanked Jesus. But how do you thank the Lord for the life of your brother? A nice card? A CD of praise music?

Then the huge significance of what had just happened would have started to sink in. Martha would have remembered that when Jesus came before the tomb to raise Lazarus from the dead, she said in front of everyone, "The smell will be really bad, because my brother has been dead for four days." And this even after Jesus had told her, quite firmly, that if she believed she would see the glory of God. I believe that Martha was the one who had the idea to buy the pound of expensive perfume of pure nard and anoint Jesus, because of what she had said to Him about the smell of death at the tomb of her brother.

And this was not just a way to say thank you. It was also saying to Jesus, "We now understand. We realize what You've been trying to tell us and the other disciples for so many months: that You will indeed be arrested, tortured, crucified, die, and be put into a tomb. But that is not the end! The tomb will not triumph! Your resurrection power will triumph over death, just as it did over the death of Lazarus! We finally get it! Your tomb will not smell of death, but it will be empty, just as our brother's now is!" Mary, Martha, and Lazarus were apparently the first of the disciples to grasp the revelation of the Resurrection of Jesus.

The text is clear: neither the twelve nor the family of Jesus had yet realized what was going to happen, despite Him having told them over and over. A check of the Gospel accounts of the Crucifixion reveals that although other Marys are present at the Cross, Mary of Bethany is not there, and neither is Martha. And looking at the accounts of the women who went to the Garden to finish the preparation of the body of Jesus for burial, we see that neither Martha nor Mary of Bethany are there. Surely Martha would have been present if there was a practical task to do for Jesus.

But she knew, as did her siblings, that the tomb would be empty. And it was. Looking beyond the angel, only a few grave clothes remained... and in the back of the tomb, just the faintest aroma of a perfume of pure nard. Jesus had understood the message: that her anointing Him was for His burial. He knew what the experts tell us today, that that amount of very pure perfume would have a lasting effect... that the aroma would stay with Him through His arrest, torture, crucifixion, and burial in the tomb. And that they realized that this symbol of the aroma of

Resurrection Life would be all that remained in the empty tomb.

This revelation of the power of Resurrection Life, as mentioned in Chapter 6, is the core of the message of missions and the life of the missionary. Without it, missions does not exist.

The third message of the perfume and the alabaster jar: when the siblings were talking over the gift of the perfume, Mary was the one who said, "Let me be the one to anoint His feet with it!" Mary would have remembered that it was she who, when Jesus asked where her brother was in order to bring him back to life, had joined in with the others to say, "Come and see." And when Jesus realized that they hadn't been able to trust Him for four days, He wept (John 11:35).

It's possible that when she saw that her actions had broken the heart of the Lord, she had for the first time, a revelation of her own sinfulness. This would also explain why two accounts exist of a woman anointing the feet of Jesus and wiping them with her hair. These accounts are so similar that certain experts say that they are the same event—and the same woman—but that John and Luke mixed them up.

But the consensus is that John wrote his Gospel decades after Luke's, in order to relate certain events that were not present, or were underemphasized, in the other three. It is unlikely that he was the mixed-up one. It's much more likely that certain of our modern theologians are the mixed-up ones!

Also, Mary of Magdala, who was almost certainly the woman of the first event (Luke 7:36-49) seems to be a very different woman from Mary of Bethany. At any rate, Luke very clearly places this event at the beginning of the ministry of Jesus, and John is definite that the event he relates takes place at the end of Jesus' ministry. And the lessons drawn from the two events are different, although possibly complementary, as we shall see.

The other interpretation of these two events is that Mary of Bethany had heard of the sinner woman of Luke 7, how she had wept over the feet of Jesus and wiped them with her tears. And Mary of Bethany might well have asked Jesus, as a "good girl" from a solid, believing family, how it was that He could have allowed such a sinner to touch Him? How could He, a Rabbi of the Pharisees, allow contact with such a woman? And Jesus would have tried to explain to her, as He did to Simon the Pharisee, that the woman loved much because she had been forgiven much. And that Simon loved Jesus little, if at all, because he thought he, as a Pharisee, had no need of forgiveness.

And Mary might have wondered about this, not seeing her need of forgiveness either. After all, she had always stayed close to her older sister Martha, who kept a close watch on what she was doing, and she had never entered into a life of sin like that woman in the house of the Pharisee. She had known Jesus her whole life, had heard the stories surrounding His birth, and had followed His ministry of proclamation and miracles closely.

And she was always overjoyed when He came to visit, in these past three years in the company of His disciples. But to need forgiveness… ? That wasn't for her, was it?

Until the day she made Him weep. She, who was so close to Him, was known already for wanting to do nothing but sit at His feet. The one who listened to Jesus. But then she realized that when crisis came to her life, she couldn't hold on to her trust in Him. She couldn't wait for four days; she broke His heart. I believe that the third message to Jesus, from Mary this time, was this: "I'm a sinner! I'm no better than that other woman! I need Your forgiveness! I have loved You little because I haven't realized how much I needed to be forgiven. But now I know it, and I come before You and these other men not as a righteous girl from an upstanding family, but as a slave, just like that other woman did. As You forgave her, please forgive me my sin." Giving the perfume, in her way, was Mary's expression of love to Jesus.

And here's the fourth message: the giving of the perfume is, at its most profound level, an expression of pure worship.

For a Biblical understanding of worship, let's go back to David and the judgment he provoked against Israel. Just as the Lord was about to prolong the judgment and destroy Jerusalem, He relented and told the angel, "Stay your hand." The angel of the Lord was standing above a hill just outside Jerusalem on the threshing floor of Ornan. David looked up and saw the angel with his outstretched sword, and he and the elders with him fell on their faces. Then the angel commanded Gad the prophet to go and tell David that he was to go and raise an altar to the Lord on that same threshing floor. So David and his elders went to that place, and Ornan saw them, and the angel also. David said to Ornan, "Sell me this site and your oxen and their yokes so I may make a sacrifice to the Lord so that the plague may be averted from Israel." Ornan replied, "If it is for the Lord, take it, it's yours." But David answered, "No, I will pay the full price; I will not offer the Lord that which costs me nothing" (I Chronicles 21:14-28).

David articulated the principle of worship: worship *costs*. And sometimes it is costly indeed. What we call "worship" is often a few minutes of song, of prayer. And those are good things, and the Lord hears and appreciates them. But does it cost us anything to "worship" in this way?

For a deeper understanding of worship, let's go back to the first place that it's mentioned in the Bible. In Genesis 22, one fine day, the Lord speaks to Abraham and says, "Abraham! Take your son, your first-born, Isaac, whom you love; and go to the land of Moriah and to a mountain which I shall show to you, and sacrifice him there to me." And Abraham did just that. No arguments, no bargaining, not even any questions.

Abraham had been so transformed from the cowardly, lying negotiator that he had been as Abram, that the Lord had to give him a new name to go with his new identity. He could have very reasonably asked the Lord, "How can You keep Your promise to bless all the families of the earth through my son, if I sacrifice him to You?" But Abraham was past all that, past trying to second-guess the Lord's plan, past hesitating before a step of obedience and faith. Abraham seems to have already decided that the Lord was utterly faithful to keep His promises, and Abraham's job was to just do what the Lord said to do, when the Lord said to do it.

On the third day of their trip, Abraham lifted up his eyes and knew instantly which hilltop was the place of sacrifice. He told the two young men he had brought with him, "Stay with the donkey; I and the boy will go over there and worship and come again to you."

What a statement! He was going to sacrifice his only son, the agent of all God's promises, and he called that worship! Abraham had learned during his long walk with the Lord that the essence of true worship is sacrifice. So he went up the mountain with the boy carrying the wood, and he found a large outcropping of rock and built the altar there. He told Isaac to lie down on top of the wood and bound him to the wood as the burnt offering.

Then he raised up his hand to strike his son with the knife, and at that point the angel of the Lord called down and cried, "Abraham! Abraham!" He was so set on obedience that the angel had to call out twice in order to stay his hand. Then Abraham lifted up his eyes and saw the ram with the horns caught in the bush, and he took the ram and sacrificed it instead of his son.

And he named that place "Jehovah-Jireh," the Lord will provide.

How could Abraham do such a thing? Because he had already known that the Lord could even raise his son from the dead, if need be, to remain faithful to His promise (Hebrews 11:17-19). So Abraham was one of the first of God's people ever to believe in the power of the resurrection.

Now, that mountain named Moriah was the same one where later the Jebusites built the city of Jerusalem, and the threshing floor of Ornan, where David sacrificed the oxen, was the same rock outcropping where Abraham built his altar to sacrifice his son. And David knew immediately that the Temple was to be built on that spot, the place of worship and sacrifice (I Chronicles 22:1).

So David gathered all the materials for the construction and left them for his son, Solomon, to build the Temple. And Solomon carried out his wishes and built the temple on the threshing floor of Ornan (II Chronicles 3:1). It became the place of worship, and of sacrifice, for God's people.

Centuries later, when the hill called, at that time, Golgotha was still part of the same mountaintop, three crosses were set up there. The Son of God was crucified on that hill between two thieves. And despite the longing of the angels to go into battle and deliver Jesus, that sacrifice was not stopped. It went on to the end, as the Son of God gave up His life—for us.

The place of historic sacrifice became the place of ultimate sacrifice, when the blood of Jesus spattered to the ground.

Worship, hope, faith, sacrifice, obedience, resurrection—all are bound up together in God's holy dance.

Is God a hard God, to require such a sacrifice from Abraham? Or even of Mary? No, because He alone is worthy of such worship. He did not stop the crucifixion of His Son, as He did the sacrifice of the son of Abraham. He gave the ultimate costly gift: the gift of His Son.

Also, those who have broken through to transformation in their understanding of Him and His plans do not see such actions as sacrifice. As Mary heard the voice of Jesus and knew that He had understood her multi-layered message, she was happy to give Him her costly gift. Abraham knew that the worst that could happen to his son would be to experience a resurrection. This is why he is recognized as the first to believe in the resurrection (Hebrews 11.17-19)! As they had their eyes fixed on Jesus, the Author and Finisher of faith, nothing else mattered so much.

Are you ready to worship, in that way? Am I?

Conclusion

Because Mary loved Jesus so much, her sacrifice was not difficult; it was the natural expression of her worship.

Some teach that the Holy Spirit helps us to obey the Lord; others say that we must just choose what is right. Both of these statements are partly true. But obedience to the Lord's commands, even to the point of sacrifice, is actually not difficult at all. The engine of obedience is love!

This foundational principle is clear in the writings of the Apostle John. In his Gospel and epistles, he links obedience and love twenty times. If we love the Lord, we will obey Him (John 14:15, 23); the ones who obey Him are the ones who love Him (John 14:21). The link is stated most clearly in I John 5:3: "This is the love of God, that we keep His commandments; and His commandments are not burdensome." If the Lord's commandments seem too hard... we do not love Him enough.

I was with one of our teams doing outreach at the Pompidou Centre in Paris, and I noticed a young man looking attentively at their skit presenting the Gospel. I went up to him afterward and asked him what he thought of the message. He said, "Oh, I've been here every afternoon this week, and I've talked to the team members. But I can't become a Christian." I asked, "Why not?" He replied, "I'm living with my girlfriend, and if I became a Christian, I would have to give that up." And he walked off.

People looking at the Christian life from outside often think it's too hard. They would have to give up too much. The steps of obedience before them seem immense because they don't love Him.

An old story illustrates this principle: A married woman had a difficult husband. Every day before he left for work, he would make a long list of chores he wanted her to do: errands to run, dishes to cook, places in the house that needed cleaning, and so on. And every evening upon his return, he would check the list. He would find the point on the list where she hadn't been able to finish because the list was so long, and he would explode in anger. This went on for a couple of years, and then he died of a heart attack (which happens to people who get angry easily).

After a time, she remarried, and her second husband was totally different. He made her no lists and didn't check up on her when he got home at night. He just loved her, and she loved him.

One day she was cleaning out a drawer and found one of the lists made by her first husband. She read it again, thinking how different her second marriage was from the first. And then she realized that now, she was doing everything on the old list, and even more! Without having to think about it or make an effort. The difference was love.

This story is a parable of the Gospel; the Apostle Paul tells it, a bit differently, at the beginning of Romans 7. A Christian is one who keeps the Law of God... without having to worry about it. After all, Jesus summed up the Law in two commandments: to love God and to love our neighbor. Paul summed it up in one word: love. The essence of the law is love, and if we love enough, obedience to all God says to do will be easy.

Why has the Church still not obeyed the Lord's Last Commandment, to go and preach the Good News to all people? Because we haven't loved Him enough. This obedience will be accomplished once our love has grown to the right level, and when it does, the obedience will not be burdensome. In the 1970s, the Holy Spirit drew the people of God into new levels of praise and worship. This movement was necessary to help us grow in our love of the Lord, so that we could prepare for the sacrifices that will accomplish the Great Commission. When will we love Him enough to do what He has wanted done for so long?

How does all this work together? The question for each of us is not, *how much faith do I want?* It is rather, *how much do I want to do everything God tells me to do?*

But it's more than that.

We do not simply ask ourselves how much we are prepared to obey God; we ask ourselves, *how much do I want to love Him?*

Hope, so crucial to our faith, stability, and perseverance, is encouraged by three things: spoken words, reading the Bible, and prayer.

Faith is grown by step after step of obedience in our long walk.

Obedience, even the obedience of sacrifice, is made easy through love. Worship is an expression of our love to God. When we fix our eyes on Him and praise Him with our lips, we tell Him of our love for Him, and the Holy Spirit pours God's love back into our hearts.

And as our love grows, the disciplines of prayer, Bible study, loving our neighbors, and sharing God's love with the world, become easier and easier. Gestures that seem sacrificial to others are joys for us. Serving God and others is not hard; it is a wonderful privilege.

A life of expressing love to God through worship is no longer about gritting your teeth, forcing yourself to be disciplined, and doing things you don't like; it's no longer about programs or schedules or doing pious things or doing things religiously.

Walking with God becomes a dance, a swirl of the banners of hope, faith, and obedience, all rooted and grounded in love: love as the motor, the practice, and the end of all that we do. Faith, hope, and love abide, these three; but the greatest is love (I Corinthians 13:13). As we worship Him more, our love grows, obedience becomes easy, our authority in faith deepens, and we can walk up to the gates of the nations and demand that they open (see Matthew 16:18-19). And so we walk into our inheritance in glory.

About the Author

Dr. Tom Bloomer obtained his B.A. degree in archeology at the University of Illinois (1972) and worked as a French translator, ladies' shoe salesman, and youth pastor before joining Youth With A Mission. In 1983, he and his wife Cynthia, responded to a call from Loren Cunningham and Howard Malmstadt to help develop the University of the Nations. A Master's degree in missiology from Wheaton College Graduate School (1987) and years of missions experience proved invaluable as he helped coordinate, refine, and improve the different UofN courses.

Dr. Bloomer completed a Ph.D. in Theology of Education at Trinity International University in 1999 and has served as the International Provost of the UofN since 2001. Teaching the Word is the primary thrust of his ministry; the challenge before him is to discover what it means to love God not just with our heart, soul, and strength, but with our minds as well.

Dr. Bloomer has lived in Switzerland for forty years with his wife, who passed away in 2012. His hobbies include aerobic history, extreme gardening, and fifth-dimensional composting. His son Philip, and daughter-in-law Amy, currently live and work in Portland, Oregon.

CINDERELLA
AND HER SISTERS

IDENTITY, AUTHORITY, AND INHERITANCE

Printed in Poland
by Amazon Fulfillment
Poland Sp. z o.o., Wrocław